THE
NEWSAGENT'S
WINDOW

Also by John Osborne

Radio Head

THE NEWSAGENT'S WINDOW

ADVENTURES IN A WORLD OF SECOND-HAND CARS AND LOST CATS

JOHN OSBORNE

SIMON &
SCHUSTER

London · New York · Sydney · Toronto

A CBS COMPANY

First published in Great Britain by Simon & Schuster UK Ltd, 2010
A CBS COMPANY

Copyright © John Osborne 2010

1 3 5 7 9 10 8 6 4 2

Simon & Schuster UK Ltd
1st Floor
222 Gray's Inn Road
London WC1X 8HB

www.simonandschuster.co.uk

Simon & Schuster Australia
Sydney

Inside artwork © Mr Bingo

A CIP catalogue record for this book
is available from the British Library.

ISBN: 978-1-84737-231-4

Typeset in Bembo by M Rules

Printed in the UK by CPI Mackays, Chatham ME5 8TD

To the newsagents of Norwich

CONTENTS

PART TWO
For sale: everything I've ever bought from newsagents' windows

PROLOGUE

I sat on the floor in my empty house in Norwich. I had nothing: no bed, no TV, no settee. The cooker only had one working ring, there was no toaster, no curtains, not even a pot to put my toothbrush in.

Two months earlier I had moved back to England after spending the last year teaching in Austria. When my placement at the school in Vienna ended, I flew home and moved in with my mum and dad again, and for the first time in my life I felt completely stuck. So far everything had been laid out in front of me – school, followed by sixth form and university. But with all of that behind me, and now that my adventures abroad were over, I had to find a job. Despite having an impressive CV, proofread by my dad, I was forced to accept the grim reality of the signing-on queue at Scunthorpe Job Centre. It felt a long way from the coffee rooms, snow-peaked mountains and opera houses of Austria. It wasn't so bad being back in my parents' home: I could help myself to food from the instantly replenished fridge, I still had friends in the area, and I was able to use my dad's computer to look at job sites while he made me cups of tea. But I knew I couldn't stay, I wanted to move on. Sitting on the bed I'd slept in since I was a child, I took out my mobile phone and texted everyone I knew in Norwich, where I had been at university. When I'd exhausted my contacts there I decided to try further afield, and left messages with friends in London, Edinburgh, Liverpool. I begged for a roof over my head – I asked friends of friends, associates of associates, anyone who might know of a possible spare room I could move into for a few months while I gave myself a chance to acclimatize and try to work out what I was doing with my life.

Molly was the only one with a positive response. She had moved to Norwich just as I was about to leave to go to Vienna, but in that short time we quickly became pretty good friends. She called me, told me she was just about to complete her MA in scriptwriting at university and planned to stay in Norwich. She explained that she hated her 'twattish' housemate and was desperate to find somewhere new to live. So desperate, it seemed, that she was even willing to live with me. Molly suggested we look at houses as soon as possible, and told me she would arrange as many viewing appointments as she could. I quite liked the idea of living with a scriptwriter, staying up late into the night with a pot of coffee, watching Woody Allen films, drinking gin while listening to the *Afternoon Play* on Radio 4. Things were looking up. The next day I caught the train to Norwich, Molly met me at the station and we went to look at our first house. Two days later we signed a contract and were told we could move in immediately.

The only problem was that the house was unfurnished. The letting agent had explained this to us, but for some reason we thought it was nothing more than a minor inconvenience. We were overexcited about moving, and had been so keen to do so that common sense didn't really come into the equation. The house seemed so perfect for us. It was in a cul-de-sac in a quiet residential area; we had a good-sized front room, an apple tree in the back garden and a pond that rippled with the chorus of frogs. Once we moved in, though, we realized what we were faced with. We had no beds, no chairs, no saucepans, and our voices bounced off the walls with no curtains and furniture to soak up the noise. We had nothing. We didn't even have shelves in our fridge, there were no light bulbs in the fittings. And then we saw an advert in a newsagent's window.

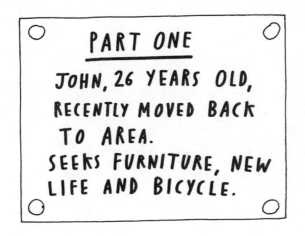

PART ONE

JOHN, 26 YEARS OLD,
RECENTLY MOVED BACK
TO AREA.
SEEKS FURNITURE, NEW
LIFE AND BICYCLE.

1

SINGLE BEDS AND A GARAGE SALE

The sign in the newsagent's window read *Two single beds for sale,
£10 each.*

'We have to have them!' Molly said.

'Are you sure?'

She nodded so I tapped the number into my mobile phone,
and was soon talking to a man about buying his beds. We had
only gone to the newsagent to buy milk, but it's amazing
how spending a night sleeping on the floor can spark you into
action.

'They're still there if we want them,' I told Molly once the
arrangements had been made. 'It's on the other side of town. I
said I'd go now.'

'Do you want me to come too?' she asked.

'Only if you want to.'

I told Molly I would see her later. Our roles had been
defined: I was hunter-gatherer; she made sure milk was in the
fridge.

*

Dan greeted me with a huge grin, and invited me inside. He wore a baseball cap and had a full, bushy beard, which with such a young face made it look as if it was held on by elastic.

'I'm getting married in two weeks,' he told me, shooing a golden retriever away from sniffing at the backs of my knees. 'No need for single beds any more!' he continued, a glint in his eye. Sadly, I wasn't in such a position – a single bed was ample for me.

The dog and I followed Dan through to his living room, where a girl wearing tartan pyjamas sat on the settee, reading *Heat* magazine.

'This is Emma,' Dan told me. 'Would you like a coffee?'

'Yes please,' we both replied, as one, and I sat down on an armchair as Dan disappeared into the kitchen.

'Are you here about the beds?' Emma asked, and I told her about the unfurnished house and the newsagent's window until Dan came back, gripping mugs with all his fingers.

'Do you want to come and have a look?' he asked, and handed me my coffee, spilling a little, treading the stain into the carpet with his socked foot as he led the way up the stairs.

'What do you think?' he asked as the door swung closed behind us. The beds were stripped bare, pushed against the back wall of the small room. Every inch of the floor was decked with sheets of newspaper, and paint pots were stacked high in the corner.

'I can finish decorating as soon as the beds have gone,' he told me. 'It's going to be a nursery, we're due to give birth in the new year.'

4

'Congratulations,' I said, and the soon-to-be father dragged the beds out so I could have a proper look at them. He sat on one, I sat on the other. I pushed down on the mattress to test for softness. It was fairly comfortable, but it didn't really matter. After spending the previous night sleeping on the floor, even if coils had been springing out I would still have handed over the cash and taken them.

The whole idea of newsagents' windows intrigued me. It seemed surprising that such a way of selling things still existed. I remember my mum and dad placing a card to sell my first bike when I was little, but that was the eighties, and I wondered why Dan hadn't posted ads online, or sold the beds on eBay.

'How long have you had them advertised for?' I asked.

'A while. A couple of months, maybe more.'

'And have many people been in contact?'

'No,' he confessed. 'Comfy?' he asked, clearly wanting to get back on track with closing his sale.

'Very,' I said, perhaps exaggerating slightly for the benefit of Dan.

'If you're interested in buying I can drive them to yours. I've got a van outside, I don't mind.'

I nodded. 'Yeah, I'll take them.' There was no way I wanted to sleep on the floor for another night, or break the news to Molly that she would have to.

'Deal!' Dan said, clearly enjoying the word as it came out of his mouth. He clapped his hands together and sprang to his feet, ready to do business. Once the twenty pounds had transferred from my pocket into his, we each took hold of an end of the first bed and set about dragging it down a narrow, steep staircase. There was a crash as a table on the landing was knocked over, birthday cards sent flying.

'Sorry!' I called out.

'Don't worry,' Dan said, not bothered about the mess, gesturing for me to continue. With both beds loaded into the back of the battered old van in the driveway, Dan called the dog with a fierce whistle to join us on our journey.

'That was a bit more strenuous than I expected!' he said, removing his baseball cap to wipe sweat from a bald patch, separated by thinning hair. 'Right, whereabouts are we heading to?' he asked, and put his hat back on. He started the engine and I hoped I'd be able to remember how to get back, not confident in my ability to direct us to my new house. My brain still hadn't adjusted to being back in Norwich after such a long time away.

We managed, only having to stop and ask for directions once, and needing just one U-turn. We jumped out of the van, and Dan helped me carry the beds back up another flight of stairs. With no other place to sit down we perched on the beds as we tried to catch our breath, unable to disguise our lack of fitness.

'Do you want a coffee?' I asked. Dan nodded, and came with me through to the kitchen. I filled up Molly's travel kettle and explained about the unfurnished house. As the kettle boiled Dan talked about his wedding, and Norwich City's disappointing season. I found out that his favourite in *Dragon's Den* was Theo, and then he explained why he had used a newsagent's window.

'A couple of years ago some dick hacked into my online banking. They wiped it clean and it was a pain in the arse to get my money back. Since then I've vowed never to buy or sell anything on the Internet again. I don't really see the need to bank online or order your shopping on the computer or chat to people on MSN. It's not that I don't trust it, or don't understand it, it's just that I prefer to do things the old-fashioned way.'

I nodded. I prefer the old-fashioned way too, and was still puzzled as to why certain technologies had to become obsolete like Walkmans, Teletext and SodaStreams.

'I should get back,' Dan said when we finished our coffees.

'Thanks for your help,' I said. We shook hands and he slapped me on the back, and what had looked like being a bleak couple of hours carrying heavy furniture with a stranger turned out to be an enjoyable, caffeine-filled morning. I moved one bed into Molly's room, the other into my own, and collapsed onto it, satisfied with a job well done, and just as I was drifting off to a daytime snooze my phone rang. It was Molly.

'I'm at a garage sale,' she told me. 'Come! Help me buy things!'

Reluctantly I got up from my bed and set off to meet her.

Norwich suburbia was leafy and warm, August was treating us well. Every house had neatly trimmed conifers, freshly cut lawns, 2.4 Mondeos on each driveway. It was just after lunchtime, a paperboy cycled past us, a fluorescent yellow bag resting on his knee as he rode without hands. I turned onto the road Molly had given me the address for, and saw a bustle outside one of the houses, with tables lining the pavement, music playing, people browsing the stalls. All it lacked was bunting, a brass band, cheese and pineapple on sticks.

'This was advertised in the same newsagent's window as the

beds,' Molly told me. 'I went back to have a look to see if there was anything else we could buy. Look at these! 10p each!' She seemed excited to be at the garage sale, making piles of plates and dishes, all mismatched patterns.

'How much money have you got on you?' I asked.

'Fifteen pounds,' she said. 'You?'

'A tenner.' In garage sale terms we were practically millionaires; anything we wanted was ours. I put a £3 toaster under my arm and carried on browsing.

A man wearing a straw hat standing behind one of the tables smiled as he saw me make a beeline for his stall. I leafed through the vinyl records and left Molly to examine crockery for cracks and fold up tea towels to add them to her pile. It wasn't long before we had bagged a couple of dining-room chairs, a proper kettle, bathroom scales, an old vacuum cleaner, two lamps and a tartan rug.

'We've just moved into a new house,' Molly explained to the woman, who looked like Victoria Wood.

'Aah, that's sweet,' she said, and neither me nor Molly had the heart to tell her we weren't newlyweds or childhood sweethearts, but were living together out of convenience, because I didn't want to live with my mum and dad, and Molly was fed up with living with a twat.

'Is there anything else you need?' she asked, as the three of us finished packing what we had stacked on the side of the road.

'Maybe cutlery?' I said, remembering one of the things we needed most urgently.

'I looked, but I couldn't find any,' Molly told me.

'Well, we've got plenty. Mike and I have more than enough.

Mike!' she called to her garage sale aide. 'It's OK if we give away a couple of bits of cutlery, isn't it?'

'Of course,' Mike said. 'Donna'll find something for you,' he boldly declared, and went back to the table he had stayed behind as long as we'd been there. Mike looked a bit like Phill Jupitus, and the boxes of records and tapes were clearly his domain. Whenever anyone joined us at the table, he would chat away about the records, tell them where he'd been when he'd originally bought the album or single, what he thought about them and that he once met the bass player.

'Anything particular, or would you like bits of everything?' Donna asked.

'Bits of everything if that's OK,' Molly said, and Donna disappeared back into the house, emerging a few minutes later with knives and forks in one hand, spoons in the other, like a Chas and Dave roadie.

'They've just moved into a new house,' she explained to Mike. To start with we had been joined by more and more browsers, but now we were the only customers.

'Is there anything else you need?' Mike asked. They had already been inside to fetch us some spare banana boxes to help pack the afternoon's purchases. Molly and I looked at each other, pretty happy with the way we were being looked after.

'We have plenty already, I think,' I said, ready to go back home.

'Well, we do need curtains,' Molly said, and I looked at her, slightly taken aback at her sudden brashness. 'The sun was so bright at five o'clock this morning. It woke me up and I couldn't get back to sleep. Curtains would be really useful.'

9

'Surely we have spare curtains somewhere?' Mike asked. 'What about those purple ones?'

'I'll see if I can find them,' Donna told us, and disappeared inside once more.

'My wife will sort you out,' Mike promised, somewhat optimistically, considering the very specific request. I went back to the vinyl while we waited for her to emerge, and before Mike had time to finish telling us about buying 'Ghost Town' by the Specials at a Cambridge record fair, the front door had swung open again.

'Here we go,' she said excitedly, a pair of curtains in her hands.

'Told you!' Mike said proudly. 'Well done, Princess.'

'I knew they would be in Emily's room somewhere,' she said. 'How are these?' she asked Molly, holding them up with both hands. 'They're a bit garish.'

They were bright and purple, with psychedelic concentric circles, the kind of curtains Janis Joplin would have had in her spare room. 'If you don't like them just say so, we won't be offended.'

'No, I *love* them,' Molly told her. 'Retro.'

Another couple joined us, from the house next door, greeted Mike and Donna warmly and started to look through the items on the tables, considerably diminished since our arrival.

'We'd better get going,' I said, and picked up one of the banana boxes.

'You've got too much to carry,' Donna said. 'Where do you live? I could give you a lift?'

'It's OK, we can walk,' Molly reassured her, 'it's not far.'

'No, let me give you a lift. You'll break your backs if you walk with all that.' She turned round to her husband, who was counting loose change in a margarine tub. 'Mike! I'm going to drive them home.'

Mike waved us a cheery farewell, Donna bleeped her Citroën Saxo unlocked and the three of us started loading banana boxes and chairs into the boot.

'We have a garage sale every year,' Donna told us on the drive home. 'We always have it on the Saturday of the August bank holiday weekend. Our daughter lives in Edinburgh, and we go and visit her every September. Both of us are retired now, and we don't make much money from the things we sell, maybe fifty pounds if we're lucky, but we use it all to take her out for a big meal. We really miss her when she's away. And over the last few years having a garage sale has turned into a nice way to get to know our neighbours. During the course of the day practically everyone will come out to say hi, look at what's on offer. We've done it for seven or eight years and didn't know anyone the first time. Now I think we know the names of people who live at every number.'

We were soon back home and out of the car, and I was grateful for the ride, the two-minute journey saved us a painful long walk, laden with crockery and bric-a-brac. We carried rugs and lamps from Donna's boot to our living room, and bit by bit our house started to feel like a home for the first time. With every teapot we removed from bubblewrap, with every cup we hung on the mug tree, we felt calmed by home comforts. Our kitchen was almost complete, cupboards were filling up, drawers were well stacked. We even had a wooden spoon, salt and pepper pots, a spatula. I switched our new kettle on. Life seems much easier when you've got a decent kettle, a couple of mugs and a box of teabags.

'Do you want a drink?' I asked, picking up the teapot, which that morning had belonged to Donna. She shook her head.

'I should be getting back to Mike really,' she told us, 'in case he's got a rush on!'

'Ooh, we still haven't given you our money,' Molly said, realizing we were almost taking advantage of the couple's good nature. 'We've got twenty-five pounds,' Molly said, getting her purse out. 'Will that be enough?'

'That's plenty,' she said, and I held out the ten-pound note from my pocket. Molly handed her the fifteen pounds, but Donna shook her head, refusing to take it.

'If you both give me ten pounds then you've both paid the same,' she said, and seemed happy to favour equilibrium over profit.

'Are you sure? I asked, thinking of their meal with their daughter, knowing an extra fiver would pay for a starter.

'Of course,' Donna said, and it was clear she wasn't going to change her mind. She seemed satisfied that her furniture and oddments had found a new home, and what had been a house full of empty, echoey rooms when Molly and I first hooked our keys onto our key rings now had a sense of history.

'Thanks so much,' Molly said once again, and waved goodbye as we showed Donna out and she drove away. Molly and I gleefully feng shuied the front room, allowing ourselves to feel proud of the afternoon's hard work, and took time to get used to our surroundings. I realized a new stage of my life was beginning. After weeks of uncertainty, I was settled down again.

I had a good feeling about living with Molly. We knew each other fairly well, but even so it was rare that it was just the two of us. Molly filled the teapot once more.

'We still need loads more stuff,' she said before the tea had even been poured, and we were faced once more with the reality of domestic necessity. 'We still need to sort out boring things, council tax, a TV, DVD player, a bin.'

'We can start all that tomorrow,' I suggested, happy to ignore real life, particularly as I was now the owner of a bed.

'No, we should sort out as much as we can today,' Molly said, 'see if we can get hold of anything else.'

I wasn't sure how I felt about living with someone who seemed so proactive; I wasn't used to this kind of decisiveness. It was early evening and shops would be closing for the day. We weren't connected to the Internet yet so couldn't buy anything online, although that seemed a less appealing option after spending the morning with Dan.

'Why don't we go and look at that newsagent's window again?' she suggested. 'That's full of weird stuff.'

'Piano lessons?' I suggested when we were back scanning the window full of cards once more. The shop had just closed for the day; the man behind the counter zipped up his jacket as he locked the door and made his way down the road.

'A massage? Golf clubs? Window cleaner?'

Molly didn't seem to appreciate my suggestions.

'Dining table?' I continued, regardless.

'Dining table?' Molly asked. 'Where?'

I pointed out the advert. Molly raised her sunglasses up to her forehead to read the card with clear vision, and was soon on her phone, making arrangements.

'We're here to see a man called Chris,' Molly said to the barman. It was Chris who was selling the dining table, and on his front door we had found a note that read *If we're not in, ask for us at the pub*. Some people have the right idea about how to live.

'Chris!' the barman called across the bar to a man on the other side of the room, who smiled, waved and beckoned for us to go over. He was with a female companion, both of them in the middle of eating a meal.

'Are you Molly?' he asked. Molly nodded. 'Just let me finish and I'll be right with you.' Chris then began spearing the remaining pieces of scampi with his fork then eating them in one mouthful, pushing discarded lettuce leaves across to the side of his plate as he chewed. The couple were perhaps in their early sixties, both dressed in short-sleeved shirts, arms bright red after the recent hot weather.

'Back in a bit,' he said to her, without allowing himself the comfort of digestion, and led us to the front door of the pub.

'We eat there every day,' Chris explained as we walked down the road back to his house. 'Every day without fail. Saves on doing shopping and washing up!'

The dining table was in the back garden, covered with a sheet of blue tarpaulin.

'Here it is,' he said, tossing the tarpaulin to one side and unveiling a table. 'We had a new table made for us by a carpenter friend a couple of months ago,' he explained. 'That's the one we use inside. I've always wanted a proper table, something beautifully made. You can't beat handcrafted furniture; it's a big passion of mine. And recently my wife and I came into some inheritance, and so we treated ourselves.'

Chris slapped the palm of his hand down on the table to show it was still sturdy. The sides had chipped edges, scuff marks and coffee cup stains, but it was perfect for our house. A dining-room table meant dinner parties. It meant Scrabble on Sunday afternoons and late-night poker games. We were going to be the best hosts in Norwich.

'We tried to give it to the charity shop,' Chris explained, 'but they didn't have any way of collecting it, and it's too heavy for us to carry there. It took long enough just to get it out here. So if you want to buy it, it's ten pounds, which we'll just take round to the charity shop, put it in their pot, then at least we're still rid of our table and they've got their money. We just thought it would be better for someone to have it rather than it standing out here. It's in good condition for its age.'

I looked at Molly and we both knew the deal had been done. I gave Chris a ten-pound note, and we took an end each, bent our knees and lifted the table. It wasn't too heavy at first, but by the end of the street we had to stop and rest. We were a long way from home and not so far in the distance we could still see the pub Chris had returned to to finish his pint.

But as we walked, despite the whitening of my knuckles, the tightening of my arms, I felt a warm feeling about the day we'd had. The people we had met had been generous and unexpect-edly friendly. Our house suddenly seemed like it was going to be a pretty special place to live. I couldn't wait to have friends over, and I knew every time I sat at the table I would think of Chris and his wife, eating every meal in the pub down the road, just as every time I made a cup of tea or used the vacuum cleaner I would think of Mike and Donna.

'So, tell me about Vienna,' Molly said when we were back home for the evening, waiting for our celebratory takeaway to be delivered, our day of spending complete. I told her about my year away, about how I lived in a cottage in the Vienna Woods. I told her about Marie, the Danish girl I met when I lived there who broke my heart. I told her about the two of us walking in the snow, collecting firewood to keep warm. My house had no central heating, so walking the Vienna Woods was a regular part of my day. Marie was spending a semester in Austria studying at university. On one of our first nights together, we spent the evening walking through the city. She had only recently moved there so I showed her around. I took her to my favourite places: the Ferris wheel, the Hofburg Palace, the banks of the Danube.

It was winter, bitterly cold, and that night more snow fell than on any night ever recorded in Austria. We circled Vienna as snowflakes the size of snowmen fell, but still we walked, hand in hand. Occasionally we would reach a path we had already taken and see our own footprints, our steps in perfect unison. We stopped a couple of times for a drink in a bar to warm ourselves up, but then we went back outside and just walked and talked and nothing had ever been more perfect. I missed my last tram home because I waited with her to make sure she caught hers, which meant I had to walk four miles back to my house. The fallen snow was as high as my knees and it got to the stage where

I was no longer walking, I was wading. When I got back the snow had risen up to the handle of the front door, and when I managed to get inside I couldn't take my shoes off because the laces were frozen, so I sat with my feet resting on an electric heater, and as I thawed myself out I thought of Marie, her long blonde hair under her woolly hat and her face red from the cold. A few months later it turned out it hadn't been just me getting cold feet, Marie moved back to Denmark, and the perfect white snow turned to sludge.

In turn Molly filled me in with gossip from Norwich, joining the dots on what had happened to our group of friends while I had been away. When she had finished telling tales of squabbles, engagements, infidelities and nights out I'd missed, she explained her reasons for wanting to move away from her old housemate so much.

'She was twenty-eight and her bed was a bunk bed. I never saw her eat anything other than fishcakes. Once, when I had a bath, she knocked on the door and asked me not to get rid of the water. You're not going to do that, are you?' Molly asked. I shook my head. Living with Molly was going to be fun, I always liked hanging out with her, and I remembered how good it can be living with your friends.

I had a question for Molly I had wanted to ask her all day.

'Do you really like those purple curtains?'

'Of course. Don't you?'

I shook my head. 'They're the most repulsive things I've ever seen.'

I wasn't convinced she was telling the truth. We went back to organizing our new house, and soon the curtains were hung, our books were on the shelves, and flowers Molly had picked from our garden were standing in the vase on the nest of tables in the centre of the room. All that was missing was a cross-stitched picture with the words *Home Sweet Home*. Which I'm sure Donna was working on for us at that moment. It was going to be an interesting few months.

2

THE MASSAGE

The first time Molly and I had stood looking at the cards outside the newsagent's window, our backs aching from sleeping on the floor, I had seen a poster advertising a massage service. It had been placed there by a woman called Lucy: aromatherapist, masseuse, podiatrist, user of newsagents' windows. Two weeks after we had been at the newsagent's, and ended up buying the single beds, I was back at the window to have a second look. In the past fortnight I had managed to find a job, working in a hotel on the other side of town, which involved working long hours and carrying heavy suitcases. But it was curiosity more than aches and pains that made me write down Lucy's phone number, and after pacing up and down outside the shop I eventually plucked up the courage to give her a call. She answered straight away, seemed really friendly, and told me forty-five minutes of relaxation would cost me £10, and so I booked an appointment for the next day.

I spent the rest of the afternoon regretting having made the call. I had never had a massage from a stranger before and wasn't really sure I should be going through with it. What troubled me was that newsagents' windows are traditionally synonymous with prostitution, *massage* often being nothing more than a euphemism for something more sinister. I wanted a massage, someone to rub my back, nothing else. But I was curious, I wanted to know more about newsagents' windows and the kind of people who used them, and it seemed the only way to find out was to respond to the advert and see what happened. Which is why, despite knowing the consequences could potentially be embarrassing and humiliating, I went ahead with the appointment, brave, bold idiot that I am.

That morning, when Molly asked if I had plans for my day, I just shook my head. I couldn't face telling her I was getting a massage from a stranger who might be a prostitute. It would be a tricky conversation to have at breakfast time. I sipped my tea in silence, wondering how the day was going to pan out. I walked to Lucy's house with overwhelming reluctance, still battling with my inner conscience of whether I should follow my instincts and phone to cancel, or be brave and face up to what I had coming to me, what kind of person she would be.

I arrived at the address and everything seemed normal. Lucy lived in a nice detached bungalow. I don't think crack dens have cobblestoned driveways. I opened the garden gate and rang the doorbell. As I waited by the 'welcome' mat on the doorstep I still half expected to be greeted by a chain-smoking prostitute wearing a dressing gown.

'Hello?'

I saw a silhouette of a face. The door only opened the width of a shoe, still on its chain.

'Hello. I've got an appointment,' I told the silhouette.

'John?'

'Yes.'

There was a clinking sound as the chain was removed and the door opened fully.

'Come in!'

I wiped my feet on the mat and stepped inside Lucy's house. The silhouette walked through to the front room, pulled a draw-string to open the curtains, and I felt my heart booming like hip hop. I started to wish I hadn't gone through with it, that turning up to my appointment had been the wrong decision. I should have stayed at home where nothing bad could happen. But now with the curtains open, daylight shone through the bay window and once Massage Lucy was revealed in full, her appearance gave my palpitations the chance to simmer a little.

Lucy was in her early fifties, and where I expected bleached blonde hair was a short brown bob, where I had imagined a low-cut top was a plain blue blouse, and where I thought I would see a miniskirt and fake-tanned bowling-pin legs was a pair of faded jeans embroidered with flowers.

'Come through, John,' she cheerfully instructed. I was still in the darkness of the hallway, and so walked through to the main room, which was proudly decorated with photographs of what looked to be her daughter's graduation ceremony. On the walls hung framed certificates honouring various yoga and massage qualifications. A widescreen television and a large collection of videos and DVDs were in one corner, with plants and pine furniture against the walls, and in the middle of the room a shelf of lotions and potions, and next to it the centrepiece: the massage table.

'Sit down, make yourself comfortable,' Lucy told me, her voice providing much needed calm. 'I've got some forms I need you to fill in before we get started.'

As I ticked the boxes on Lucy's forms I breathed a sigh of relief at the way the morning had turned out. Lucy seemed friendly, and it seemed like it was going to be a perfectly ordinary massage after all. I don't think prostitutes pay this kind of attention to administration.

'Take off your top and trousers,' Lucy said once she had my medical details and the identity of my next of kin. It was good to know a masseuse would be contacting my dad if I didn't make it through the session. I pictured the expression on his face and started to giggle a little, my nerves all over the place.

'Socks too,' she continued, and I tried to repress my smile. I unbuttoned my shirt, took off my socks and, lastly, cautiously removed my trousers.

'I . . .'

'Shush,' Lucy said, raising a finger to her lips. It was too late to turn back. 'Make yourself comfortable,' she said once more, somewhat optimistically, as I stood in front of her wearing nothing but turquoise boxer shorts from Debenhams. 'Pop yourself on the table,' she said, tapping the surface like I was a Jack Russell.

I lay down and, never having had a massage before, was as relaxed as if I had been about to receive a vasectomy without anaesthetic performed by Ozzy Osbourne. Massage Lucy manoeuvred me as though my limbs were made of Plasticine so that my shoulders and neck were hanging off the edge of the table. This was not comfortable.

'Are you comfortable?'

'Yes.'

Lucy put a CD into her stereo, rubbing her hands with oils as birdsong came out of the speakers. There is nothing relaxing about music simulating Amazonian rainforests.

'Are you relaxed?' she asked.

'Yes.'

'What do you do for a living?'

'I've just started work in a hotel,' was the response I tried to squeeze out, but my answers could be nothing more than short and muffled. I found it difficult to talk as my head was buried in a pillow; I felt more horizontal than I had ever been before and was very aware I wasn't wearing any clothes.

'What you must realize,' Lucy told me, 'is that as soon as my hands touch your skin, I will know all about you in intimate detail. I have a special relationship with my clients, I get to know all about their lives, just by touch. So relax,' she told me, 'listen to the music, let it take you on a peaceful journey.'

Despite the lavender-scented candles and what was now soft, lulling piano music, I had a thousand thoughts running through my mind, so making it go blank was not easy, which Lucy seemed aware of straight away.

'Breathe with me if you like,' she suggested. 'In . . .' I copied her exaggerated rhythms, 'and out, in . . .' she motioned for me to keep up with her, 'and out.' Eventually my ribcage relaxed and so too did my shoulders, spine, wrists and hips, and I was able to stop worrying and began to believe there was a chance I could actually enjoy the next forty-five minutes.

The period of blissful relaxation lasted no more than thirty seconds. It was interrupted when Lucy started a patacake slapping of my back as my eyes opened again and my neck tensed.

'Julius Caesar had this done to him every day of his life!' she told me, raising her voice to make herself heard above the din of the smacking. 'If it was good enough for him . . .' she said, and the rest of the statement disappeared with the sensation of my skin being slapped. When she finished whacking me she started a more violent rhythmical drumming of my back with the balls of her fists.

'This will sting,' she warned me. Already I was in some pain and I didn't welcome the thought of more stabbing sensations.

'The blood . . .' she explained, and I almost bolted upright at the sound of the word, 'should flow around more freely now.'

I stayed where I was, relieved that the rest of the sentence was not '. . . the blood will stop pouring out of your spine soon.'

'You need to relax more. In and out, in and out. Breathe, relax, breathe, relax.' I felt like I wouldn't ever be able to breathe or relax again.

By the end of the session my head had flopped forward, my eyes were closed, and I had almost fallen asleep, a trail of slobber dribbling from the corner of my mouth. I had rediscovered the art of breathing and felt quite disappointed when the forty-five minutes were over, when Lucy switched off the music and started to towel-dry her hands. I had only just perfected the second of her commands, to relax, and was beginning to realize the benefits of having a massage, but it was too late. I sat upright and wiped my eyes, trying to wake myself up.

'Your shoulders are incredibly tense,' Lucy said to me as I dangled my legs over the edge of the massage table. She put her hands on my back once more, rubbing an area just below my neck which felt particularly tender. 'You are not a confident person,' she continued. She stopped rubbing, and walked across the room, where she poured a glass of water from a carafe and placed it on the table beside me. 'The blood in your lower back is not flowing as it should,' she told me as I took a sip. 'This is because you are a "yes" person. You like to please people and it is often at your own expense. *You* should be your own number one priority, but you are down at the bottom. This means that one day you will explode and have some kind of breakdown.'

I looked up. Lucy nodded. 'You will explode,' she repeated, and I pictured myself in a few years standing on the central reservation shouting at motorway traffic, or going ballistic at a waitress for telling me I couldn't have a Frappuccino because the machine was not working.

'Frustration is bubbling up inside you and it is not healthy,' Lucy continued. 'One day it will all be released. Anger needs to be let out gradually, little by little, but you are not doing this. You bottle things up. You are not decisive enough. You see other people with confidence and you feel envious of them, you like to watch them perform. You wish you could be more assertive. You struggle with relationships, there is no one close to you right now. You have no soulmate. You have no goals any more. You have run out of dreams. This is why you do not sleep well at night.' She paused, waiting for the information to be digested. 'Do you mind me saying all of this?'

I shook my head, but I wanted her to stop, all of this seemed terrifying, mainly because it was so accurate. It was unnerving that we had only known each other for an hour, that I had barely said anything to her.

'You can tell all this from my shoulders?' I asked, taking another sip of water.

'As soon as I touched your back I knew more about you than you could imagine. Just like I warned you.' Although Lucy's words seemed foreboding, her voice was kind, her concern genuine. 'You have been taking on too much. You have no one to worry about you. Well, I am going to worry about you now. I will be Mum number two.'

She handed me the leaflet I had originally seen in the window of the newsagent and a business card.

'You should come back to me for reflexology,' she said. 'Everyone should have reflexology. It should be available for free on the NHS. Also, I am a clairvoyant and deal with the spirit world. It was the spirits who guided you here today.' After all Lucy had just told me the cynic inside me had fallen silent. Sat on her settee, I was mesmerized and found myself perfectly willing to accept the spirits had taken me by the hand that morning and guided me through the streets of Norwich and up onto her massage table.

I looked at her as she spoke to me, and tried to take everything in. I was experiencing one of the most bizarre, intense, intrusive moments I had ever known; a complete stranger was telling me more about my life than I knew myself and all I could do was sit there listening, while wearing nothing but turquoise boxer shorts. Massage Lucy willed me to change and I knew she was right.

I thought about all the frustrations and anxieties that had built up inside me. My life did need to improve, this seemed the right time to put things right. I couldn't continue the way I had been.

'If you want to change you need to start saying no to things,' she continued. 'Start letting people down,' she said, each instruction punctuated by a clap of her hands. 'People are strong enough to take it. Don't put so much burden on yourself. Don't think about things so much. Don't analyse things. Don't say yes to things you would rather say no to. Drink more water, eat healthily, swim. Phone me, ask if you need help. Confide in someone. Don't be scared to shout and scream occasionally, let it all out, it's so important to get things off your chest. But most importantly, make sure you come back and see me again so I can check up on you, see how you're doing.'

I finished my water, put the empty glass on a coaster on her coffee table and picked up my trousers from the heap I had left on the floor, my heart racing once more. I pulled the trousers on, fastened my belt, buttoned my shirt. Yet it had not been displaying my body that had left me feeling exposed and vulnerable.

'Thank you,' I said to Lucy as I made my way back outside.

'You're welcome,' she said. I paid her the ten pounds and promised I would follow her advice.

'Make sure you come back!' she called after me as I walked away.

I called back that I would, and promised myself it wouldn't be long until I saw her again, when I would be a much improved human being.

I couldn't be sure whether it was Lucy's massage or her advice that had made me feel so perky on my way home. I went to the supermarket and revelled in the freshness of the fruit and veg aisle. Back home, I ate half a bag of satsumas and stacked the fridge with bottles of Evian. At work, staff were allowed to use the swimming pool, so the next day after my shift I went down there. I dived into the pool and swam, and swam. I didn't count my lengths as I would normally have done, I just swam until I was exhausted, achieving a completely blank mind, as Lucy had instructed. Afterwards I spent twenty minutes in the Jacuzzi, making sure that all the stress I'd accumulated during my shift would disappear by the time I got into the shower so that I wasn't carrying around any tension inside. Already I was enjoying this new lifestyle. I looked forward to being invited out to the pub when I didn't really want to go, or being phoned by a Vodafone salesman. I would say no, when once I'd have said yes, and make Massage Lucy proud.

The one observation that Lucy had not hit the bull's-eye with was when she said she knew I did not sleep well at night. She was wrong, I genuinely did sleep well most nights. But I didn't the night after I went for my massage, I just stared at my bedroom ceiling trying to work out what had happened, trying to retrace the way she had got into my mind. I knew that she had probably been saying things so generic that they could be recognized by anyone. I knew how these things worked, I'd watched Derren Brown. But even so, she had hit some home truths that had stuck with me. It had been a good idea to meet Lucy, but I never imagined it would turn out the way it had. I had learned a lot: not to worry about other people, to take more care of myself, but most of all not to jump to conclusions about masseuses.

3

PETE'S VIDEOS

When I booked the appointment with Massage Lucy, it had been with the intention of finding out about the kind of person who would advertise something so morally ambiguous in a newsagent's window. I realized, however, that I had barely learned anything about Lucy at all. I knew that she gave massages, that she liked reflexology, that her daughter had graduated, and that she had nice warm hands. But the person I had learned more about had been myself, or at least a version of myself that had been evaluated and judged by a stranger. Our conversation had made me recognize I was ignoring important things in my own life. I was putting on weight, losing contact with friends, single. My health and relationships had been neglected in favour of . . . well, nothing at all really. But since meeting Lucy I felt a real urgency to be more decisive. My main motivation for moving back to England rather than staying on teaching in Vienna had been the constant feeling I was missing out on something. I worried that my friends were all moving on with their lives while I was treading water, hundreds of miles away, like the one remaining suitcase going round and round on an airport carousel. I came back expecting to see the same Norwich I had left, but so much had changed in a year. A lot of my friends, newly graduated, had moved away. Those who had stayed were getting married, buying homes, having babies. Others had a foot on the corporate ladder and were in well-paid jobs that sent them to business meetings in places like Cheltenham and Stevenage. I didn't like the fact that none of us were students any more, that other people were getting on with their lives while I didn't have a clue what I was doing with mine. It seemed that Massage Lucy had recognized this, had thrown me a rope and was reeling me in.

It was this sense of alienation, of feeling the need to start again that meant I carried on meeting people through newsagents' windows. It felt the right thing to do, I wanted to find out more about the area I lived in, the people I walked past every day. And it would be good to do more activities, meet new people, try to replace the friends that had left. Our house was still pretty bare. Whenever I passed a newsagent I would take a moment to read the cards, looking for something extra: a mirror for the bathroom or a desk for my bedroom. I started to vary my route home from work at the hotel, knowing if I went a slightly longer way I'd pass different newsagents. And it was in a window near the hotel that I saw an advert for a video player and fifty films for £50. This was tempting. An address was written on the card, but I couldn't read it, the ink was smudged and the handwriting was barely legible. I did my best to form a semblance of what the address could be, and walked round to what I hoped was the right place.

I went to a block of flats straight out of a Mike Leigh film, storey after storey of dank grey concrete. I walked up two flights of steps, passed teenagers on rollerblades and tinny drum and bass coming out of cheap speakers, and knocked on the front door, rang on a doorbell that didn't work, knocked again, and after a while the door opened.

'I've come about the videos,' I explained. The man who answered seemed confused, and I wondered if perhaps I had woken him. 'Are you selling videos?' I asked, aware of the possibility that I was baffling someone. To my relief he nodded and opened the door for me to come in. He seemed a little timid, introduced himself as Pete, and shook my hand. He wore a bright-orange tattered polo shirt with the logo of a building company across its chest. We walked inside and I was slightly taken aback to see that his whole accommodation was one room – a single bed, kitchen units, a grimy work surface and sink. On the floor were a couple of empty wine bottles, next to them an ashtray, the carpet surrounding it stained with fag ash. The room smelt of stale tobacco, a pungent tang that would take more than a few opened windows and a squirt of air freshener to get rid of. Tossed on the floor were newspapers, weekend tabloid supplements with selected programmes on the TV guide marked in blue highlighter. The *Channel 4 News* blared out of a staticy portable television, and Pete stooped to turn the volume down, leaving me and Krishnan Guru-Murthy looking around the bedsit in awkward silence.

The videos Pete had advertised were stacked high against the wall. I tried to scan the titles on the cases as he hurriedly tidied bits of his home. He seemed flustered at having a visitor, my presence panicked him, and he threw his duvet back onto his bed, kicked scattered laundry out of sight. But the mess didn't bother me. I was excited by the videos, I really wanted to buy them. All my life I've been surrounded by people referencing films, talking about specific scenes, actors, directors, but it's always gone over my head. I've never seen *Star Wars* or *The Lord of the Rings*, I've never seen *Indiana Jones* or *The Godfather*. I didn't see *Ghostbusters* until I was twenty-five, which admittedly seems a bit pathetic. I don't generally have the patience to watch films, anything longer than an episode of *Neighbours* and I'm dozing like a pensioner on Christmas afternoon. And as a result I couldn't help but feel left out when I was with more cinema-savvy friends. I've seen *Home Alone* twice but that never really made up for it. It wasn't like I'd spent the time I'd saved reading Booker Prize winners or brushing up on my French past participles or learning to play the bass. I don't know why my life has been so absent of films – perhaps it's because I never had an older brother to watch films with, or because I never had one of those friends at school my parents would have disapproved of, who would show me horror movies as we smoked out of the bedroom window. But now Pete had unwittingly turned into that older brother I never had, the cool friend with a stash of cigarettes, stubbies of beer and a big film collection. Without realizing it, Pete had achieved every schoolboy's dream. He was allowed a TV in his bedroom.

The possibility of getting my hands on so many unseen films was pretty exciting. Maybe once I'd watched them all, I'd be in the pub and someone would make a reference to something I had seen, and I would feel triumphant, I wouldn't feel left out any more. And it would be all down to Pete. It wasn't so much for myself that I was responding to the advert in the newsagent's window, it was more for that fifteen-year-old me, who had never seen *Back to the Future*.

Among Pete's films were a few comedies which didn't really sit comfortably in the horror-dominated collection. Between *The Unholy* and *Werewolf* was *Unseen Mr Bean*. Mixed up with *The Silence of the Lambs* and *Thirteen Ghosts* was *Kevin and Perry Go Large*. Something that really stood out was a box set of both series of *The Young Ones*.

'I love *The Young Ones*!' I said to Pete, picking the cases up to read the inlays.

'I only bought those two weeks ago,' he told me, picking up the first of the two cases. 'I don't think I've ever laughed as much as the couple of days I spent watching those episodes.'

This was the first time Pete had really spoken, and I started to feel bad. I couldn't help but think of him on his own in his bedsit, roaring with laughter to *The Young Ones*, to Neil becoming a policeman and trying to break up a rave by shouting: 'It's the pigs.' I could imagine Pete, cigarette in hand, slightly pissed on red wine, chuckling to Mike hammering plates to the table, at Rick's rants against Thatcher. I started to feel guilty at the thought of taking something away from Pete that he clearly would have preferred to keep. I looked at it from his point of view, how he would have felt about me turning up and going through his video collection. Even though he had advertised it in a newsagent's window, maybe this wasn't what he wanted. I thought about how I would feel if I was in financial trouble and someone came to my house to take away my *Seinfeld* box sets. It would break my heart. Maybe this was the wrong thing to do.

One of my problems, as Massage Lucy had pointed out to me, is that I feel sorry for people. I visualize situations too much, I can't help it. At work, if a guest asked something as simple as whether their spectacles had been handed in, I always felt for them, pictured them squinting, booking an appointment with the optician, their life temporarily hampered because they couldn't find their glasses. If someone came to the reception desk and complained about their room, or expressed disappointment at their evening meal, I would feel really sorry for them; it would ruin the rest of my shift. So a man selling his entire video collection by advertising in a newsagent's window meant it was hard not to think of how, and why, and the resonance it must have had for him.

Pete took the second *Young Ones* video from me and had a look himself.

'I missed out when it was on TV originally,' he said, tapping the video case with the knuckles of his right hand.

'How much did you want for all these?' I asked.

'I wrote fifty pounds on the card,' Pete replied. He spoke with a thick Norfolk accent, and his voice was so quiet I had to strain to make out what he said.

Fifty pounds seemed a reasonable amount, especially as the films were ones I wanted to see, *From Dusk Till Dawn*, *Pulp Fiction*, *Interview with the Vampire*. I had planned on implementing a hard-ass business acumen and only offering £20, particularly in light of the advice from Massage Lucy to look after myself and not be overly concerned with the feelings of other people. But I didn't have the heart to do it to Pete, who was sat in his chair, scratching his stubble. I hope Lucy would have understood my leniency.

I gave him the £50, and he started to put his videos into a bin bag for me. I couldn't help but feel like a bailiff. The videos were the only personal possessions that I could see in his flat, apart from the ashtray, the bottles of wine. I looked around: there were no books, no pictures, no mementos, no photographs. I tore off a second bin bag from the reel and started to fill it with the remaining videos. Pete unplugged his VCR and put it on the pile for me to take. Already we were on a third bin bag; as Pete started passing me blank videos I realized I was also getting anything he had randomly taped off the telly. He was getting rid of videos with handwritten stickers, *Mad Max 3*, *Die Hard 2*, *Jurassic Park*, *The Crow*, and tape after tape of unlabelled videos. Suddenly it wasn't just films I was buying, it was little pieces of his life.

I was aware it was a perfectly fair transaction, where both parties walked away with what they had asked for, but I wondered whether perhaps this was an advert I should not have answered. With a bin bag under each arm, I said goodbye to Pete, but couldn't face making eye contact as I left his bedsit. I decided that watching every video I had inherited from him was the only way I could justify taking them away with me. It didn't matter if I'd seen it before or whether I thought I would like it or not. I would watch *Gladiator*. I would watch *The Dentist 2: Brace Yourself*. I would watch *How to Take Up Coarse Fishing*, I would even watch *Braveheart*. I couldn't wait to get the videotapes home, hooking up my little portable telly to Pete's VCR – the most lo-fi cinema system possible to put together.

The bin bags started to rip before I had even got to the bottom of the stairs in the block. I didn't want to leave a trail of videos behind me, like breadcrumbs leading back to Pete's place,

so I called a taxi. There were clearly more than the fifty videos
Pete had advertised, the figure was closer to a hundred, if not
more. As I waited for the taxi to arrive I wondered how Pete
would be spending the rest of his evening, how he felt about
losing all his videos. I wondered what he would do with his fifty
pounds. What had seemed like a big sum of money when I
took it out of the cash machine seemed paltry now.

'What have you got there?' the taxi driver asked. It wasn't an
unreasonable question, I'd just covered his back seat with ripped
bin bags. Whether through a feeling of guilt, or because it would
have been too hard to explain, I decided to resort to a lie.

'My friend's moving house and he's given me all his videos.'

That definitely sounded like a lie. The driver seemed interested and had a look for himself.

'I've got a pretty big video collection myself,' he said as he
stopped the engine. 'Seems a waste now. Hundreds of pounds of
videos. Thousands maybe. Just taking up too much space.'

I started to worry I'd end up buying the taxi driver's videos
too. Maybe I should have started a house clearance service.

'Enjoy the films,' he said as I got out of the taxi and made my
way inside. It was still early evening, I had the house to myself and
didn't have to be at work until the following afternoon. It looked
like I had a late night of watching videos ahead of me. Sympathy
for Pete had been overwritten by the prospect of watching films
I had never seen. I unpacked the videos from the bin bags and
made a stack of them against the wall, almost reaching to the ceiling. I connected Pete's VCR and settled down, starting with the
video at the top of the pile. You can tell a lot about someone by
going through a random video from their collection, but it's not so

much what they have chosen to record, it's the flickering bits from the video's previous incarnation, the programmes recorded on a bored afternoon because there was a spare half an hour of blank space at the end.

I put one of the unlabelled videos into the VCR and watched it in fast forward, the contents flashing before my eyes: Del Boy and Rodney dressed as Batman and Robin merged into Jack and Vera in *Coronation Street*. The video spanned perhaps twenty years, a life of pressing record. Michael Fish . . . static . . . *Big Brother's Little Brother* . . . adverts . . . an old *Match of the Day*. These were all programmes I watched, the extent to which I resembled Pete was starting to get a bit eerie. I didn't want to turn into him, to be as isolated as he seemed to be. So I decided to watch all of these anonymous videos too. I would never tape over them, they were Pete's videos, not mine.

I thought that if I didn't do as Massage Lucy had advised, maybe all this would be coming my way in the future. It might be me living in a bedsit with no photographs on the mantelpiece, no pictures on the walls. When Lucy told me there were spirits looking after me I knew it wasn't true, but it did make me think. Perhaps in his own way Pete was a ghost of my future, how I might turn out if I didn't look after myself better. I put a new video in the machine, pressed play, but couldn't concentrate on the film. All I could see was myself in turquoise boxer shorts, sitting on Lucy's settee.

4

————

THE YOGA CLASS

Every Thursday a man called James Lewis runs yoga classes in a Norwich sports hall. I've seen it advertised in newsagents' windows across town, so decided to go along and see whether his yoga was as good as his marketing.

It wasn't just because I had seen the card that I was going. Looking at the array of adverts offering different clubs and activities, I recognized that I didn't really have any hobbies any more. There had become little reason to leave the house other than to go to work. Yoga seemed a good enough way as any to spend an evening, and I was determined that Massage Lucy would see me in much better condition the next time I went round there. I wanted to be more healthy for her sake as much as my own. I fully intended to go and see her in a few months' time and show her the dramatic improvement I had made in my life. I wanted her to see that I had stopped saying 'yes' to things I wanted to say 'no' to. Yoga was one of the forms of exercise she had recommended. She said it would be therapeutic for me, help me unwind from the stresses of working in a hotel. I had been taken by surprise at how chaotic it was, how rude people were, how many unreasonable complaints I had to deal with, how many utter bastards I had to tolerate. Anyone who works in a stressful job needs to exercise, be healthy, and yoga helps maintain a tranquillity in life, which is why, when I saw the advert in the newsagent's window, I decided to go along. And I thought it would be funny.

The lesson started at six o'clock. As I neared the sports hall I started to spot fellow yoga enthusiasts. I could see a woman wearing an Umbro tracksuit with a sports bag over her shoulder. In the car park I saw a woman in a car give the driver a kiss on the cheek and he waved as she walked inside. It reminded me how activities play such a big part in people's lives. I hadn't been part of anything like that since I was at school, when I had Chess Club on Mondays, football practice on Wednesdays, swimming lessons on Fridays. For some families around Norwich, Thursday was the night Dad had to cook the tea because 'Mum's at yoga'. All over the country, people like James Lewis organize activities for which people arrange lifts, delay housework or homework, and put their daily routine on hold for a couple of hours.

This was the everyday life I had forgotten existed because I had spent too much time in the slightly altered realities of university life and then living abroad. I was pleased at doing something more adventurous than I would do normally on a free Thursday evening, when I would usually play football in my living room with a pair of balled-up socks.

'Am I in the right place for yoga?' I asked a man in a leotard, although the question seemed unnecessary as the people I could see stretching and limbering up had slender physiques that suggested they weren't there for rugby practice.

'Is this your first time here?' the man asked, his question equally unnecessary. When I introduced myself, he wrote my name on the register. He told me he was James Lewis and that I could pay him six pounds. I glimpsed the names on the register as I counted out pound coins into his cupped hand, and realized I would be the only new boy; all the other names had a string of ticks in the attendance column which dated back weeks and weeks. Other people were going to be in much better shape than me. This could be embarrassing.

'Follow me,' James Lewis said, and I went with him through to the main hall. There were nine others in the class, all of them female and closer to my mum's age than my own.

'Have you not got your own mat?' he asked. I shook my head and he seemed surprised, slightly annoyed even, and I wondered whether it had been stipulated in the advert. He disappeared through a side door and emerged with a blue crash mat, something that is as much a part of sports hall furniture as the track marks of the basketball court and the wooden benches which lined the walls. The sound of the mat dragging across the floor brought back memories of PE lessons and rainy playtimes, schoolbags heavy with sports kit and stinking trainers.

I felt relaxed, considering I was about to spend the next ninety minutes bending over in front of strangers. My expectations were not high, all I wanted was to not look an idiot; that is what I ask of yoga and what I ask of life. Just as James Lewis was about to begin the lesson, he noticed something amiss.

'John!' he called out from his position at the front of the class, beneath a basketball hoop. His voice echoed around the sports hall and I looked up, thinking he was perhaps calling out the register. He was pointing at his own bare feet.

'We take our shoes and socks off for yoga.'

As I bent down to untie my shoelaces I knew people were looking at me and was very aware that they were all looking at the same thing – I was wearing bowling shoes. When I left the house that morning I had not realized my final destination would be a yoga class. It had been a spur of the moment decision. I had seen an advert and so turned up at the sports hall. If I had known I was going to be doing exercise I would have worn something a bit more practical than jeans and a jumper. And I certainly would not have worn my bowling shoes.

A couple of months earlier I had been ten-pin bowling with some friends. We decided to go on a weekday afternoon, as it was cheaper to go off-peak and there would be no kids running amok. It was a good plan, which we executed perfectly, except that we were unaware it was the half-term holidays. The place was full of gangs of teenagers and fully booked, so while we waited for a lane to become free we went to the bar.

After a couple of hours of drinking Grolsch, a lane became available, and we went to play. It was only once we'd left the bowling alley I realized I was still wearing the bowling shoes. I could have gone back to exchange them, I was only a few minutes down the road, but decided to persevere with what I had rather than return them. I liked my new bowling shoes. They were considerably less battered and smelly than my old trainers, which now belonged to Millennium Bowl in Norwich.

I occasionally wore the shoes when I went out, they were somehow much more comfortable than shoes I already owned. The
people at yoga were not to know this, however, and as I untied
the laces and stuffed my socks inside my stolen bowling shoes
I thought of how much contempt I would have for anyone I saw
wearing the same footwear. Embarrassed, I tried to persuade
myself that no one was judging me, that nobody was watching
me, and if they were it would be my bare yellow feet that
disgusted them rather than my choice of pumps. Once I had
sorted myself out, James Lewis instructed us to lie down on our
mats. Soon we were horizontal, stretching our legs as fully as we
could, raising our arms high in the air.

'Close your eyes,' he instructed the class. 'Allow your muscles
to relax, your limbs to loosen.' Just like my experience with
Massage Lucy I found it difficult to relax on command. It took
a while for me to be able to feel the sensation of relaxation. I felt
I was infiltrating a meeting of grown-ups.

Once James Lewis was satisfied our muscles were at peace
with the world, he told us to stand up, and when we had all
got to our feet he told us how to perform a sun salutation. He
demonstrated what we were to do, then talked us through each
stage, raising our arms like sunflowers, emerging from a crouched
position until we were on the tips of our tiptoes. I felt like I was
in S Club Juniors. I managed to keep pace with the others in my
group even though they had all been to yoga class before. This
was easy, I was a natural. We repeated the sun salutation without
needing to take the lead from our choreographer, and soon were
saluting it with ease.

We dismissed the sun as quickly as we had saluted it and our next task was the art of balancing. James Lewis demonstrated how to stretch out an arm like a lollipop man and bring the toe of your right foot up to the inside of the left groin. I didn't like the look of it, as my balance is poor at the best of times. I can barely walk in a straight line, never mind balance with a foot in my groin.

'If you haven't done yoga regularly you may struggle with this,' James Lewis told the group but I could tell he was aiming it directly at me. I was clearly the only newcomer, and was struggling to simulate a man who knew what he was doing. I had noticed that after a bright start I was already starting to lag behind, and suspected I was getting everything wrong. I stumbled around on one leg for a little while and then gave up while the rest of the class continued with the exercise, graceful on the comfort of their own mats. James Lewis looked at me, disappointed. He knew I was not going to be his Daniel LaRusso and that he would never be my Mr Miyagi. I had failed, but at least I failed graciously.

'Forget your mind and you'll be free,' James Lewis said to us. One of the purposes of yoga is to relax your mind, to rid it of all negative thoughts and to be at complete peace with yourself. But it's difficult to forget your mind; being relaxed isn't easy in a public place when you haven't got your socks on. From very early on I knew that this was likely to be my one and only attempt at yoga; as soon as the lesson ended that would be the end for myself and Señor Zen. It was slightly frustrating that I couldn't do it. I liked the idea of being naturally good at yoga, of practising it at home, stretching and gurning at six every morning. It would have been good to be able to wrap my legs around the back of my neck while listening to *Today* on Radio 4, salute the sun as it was rising, wave at it like a kid on a boat trip. I liked the idea of owning my own mat. I would put stickers on it and find a special place to keep it in my bedroom. But just like learning to play guitar and reading Chekhov, yoga was clearly something I would never master.

'The next exercise is a difficult one,' James Lewis told us after another spell of stretching, touching toes and aligning spines. 'If you don't feel comfortable doing it where you are, feel free to use the wall.'

Our leotarded instructor put his head on his mat and started to demonstrate a manoeuvre that looked impossible to anyone with vertebrae.

'Please use the wall if you feel it would help you,' he reiterated while upside down.

Practically all the class moved to the wall, keen to take the easy option. The only person who decided to stay where she was and take what was coming to her was the girl in front of me – the girl with the straightest back in class, the best posture, the sparkliest mat. She was the girl who never had stabilizers on her bike, who never needed bumpers when she went ten-pin bowling, who could always get the ball through the windmill during crazy golf. I'm sure I saw her give James Lewis a shiny green apple at the beginning of class. As our snazzy tutor focused his attention on her, the rest of us lay flat on our backs, our heads touching the wall as we attempted to flip our legs over so that the soles of our feet would touch the brickwork. This was not relaxing. We were told the name of this exercise, which proved to be the penultimate of the lesson, but I have no idea what it was. Perhaps this is because I was so involved in the moment. But really I know it's just because I've not got a very good memory.

The final exercise of the class was the corpse position. This was where we lay on our backs, relaxed our limbs, made our wrists and ankles go floppy, and for a minute of our lives we were told to pretend we were corpses. I quite enjoyed it. As I relaxed, supine on my crash mat, I tried to make my mind go blank. I closed my eyes and used Massage Lucy's breathing technique, pretending she was with me, instructing me to breathe in and out, in and out. Perhaps yoga wasn't as bad as I had thought, maybe I should come again for another session, maybe I would get better at it. I started to realize that I had adopted the wrong attitude towards the class. Unlike other activities I'd done, this was not about who was the best, who could swim the quickest length, who could be awarded the most badges, who could curl in the best free kick. I had approached yoga the wrong way, it was about something I wasn't particularly familiar with – being at peace with yourself, making your mind go blank, the ability to be completely relaxed and escape the monotony of everyday life. I wondered whether others in the class, lying on the floor of the sports hall pretending to be a corpse had managed to make their minds go blank. Or whether, like me, they found it difficult to stop themselves thinking about work and the bad things that had happened in the day.

My time in the hotel was more stressful than I could have imagined. When I taught English to schoolkids in Vienna I had to stand in front of class after class of unenthusiastic children who spoke a different language from me, but that was like

45

drinking champagne in a Jacuzzi compared with sitting behind a reception desk and dealing with businessmen. It was hard work taking endless complaints from people unhappy with their rooms, trying to help out coach parties, giving directions over the phone. It was my first experience of working in the service industry and I realized how tough it is. I had found teaching fun – my duties were rarely more complex than sitting with sixth formers and talking about last night's TV or telling eleven-year-olds the names of animals. I woke up every morning looking forward to going to work. That's a pretty rare luxury and one I hadn't managed to recreate at the hotel. I didn't feel comfortable dealing with complaints and arguments and having raised voices directed at me. These are things I have spent my whole life trying to avoid. That's why the happiest few minutes of my whole day were when I had my eyes closed, and was lying on the floor of a sports hall, in a room full of strangers, pretending to be a corpse.

Once we had awoken from the dead, it was time for those who had brought mats with them to roll them up and tuck them under their arms, time for those who had been wearing bowling shoes to put them back on, feeling more relaxed and healthier. James Lewis said goodbye to us and the group filtered out to the car park where husbands in Vauxhalls were waiting to give lifts back home.

'Thanks for that, James,' I said as he walked past me to switch off the lights and lock up.

'John, thanks for coming. See you next week?' he asked, but I knew he didn't expect to see me again, and I imagined he was probably right. As I set off down the road away from the sports hall I heard a girl call out my name. I turned around and it was a woman who had been in my class. I didn't have a clue what she wanted. Maybe she had been impressed by some of my moves. Certainly she had been impressed enough to remember my name. Although in fairness 'John' isn't particularly tricky. Maybe she wanted some advice about how she could improve her own yoga. She pointed at the ground behind me.

'You dropped a fiver,' she said.

'Oh,' I replied, and saw it gently disappearing out of reach, being taken away by the breeze. 'Thanks!' I called after her, and felt genuinely relieved as I stooped to pick it up and pocket it.

'That would have been an expensive yoga class!' she said with a smile as she got into her car. I thanked her as I walked away, slightly humbled at her honesty. I carried on with my journey and felt pretty positive about life. I had survived the yoga class without looking too stupid, and I felt I'd earned the right to feel good about myself. After my encounter with Massage Lucy I had felt a very odd sense of unease. It had unsettled me and made me re-evaluate completely what I was doing with my life. But this had actually made me feel a little more relaxed, and as I got back to my house I acknowledged that perhaps I had just experienced the magical effects of yoga.

'What have you been up to?' Molly asked, checking her emails at the dining table.

'I've been to a yoga class,' I told her, trying to feign nonchalance.

'Yoga?'

'Yoga.'

'Why?'

I couldn't lie to Molly. She knew there was no way I would go to yoga class under normal circumstances. I didn't lead a healthy lifestyle. She'd seen the way I behaved with a multipack of McCoy's crisps.

'I saw it advertised in a newsagent's window,' I admitted.

Molly laughed; it was clearly something she thought was a bit stupid. 'How was it?'

'A bit scary,' I replied, still surprised I had actually gone through with it.

'You should have told me, I'd have come with you. I'd like to go to a yoga class.'

I hadn't even thought about inviting anyone to come along with me. Maybe I'd have enjoyed it more if I'd gone along with one of my friends. But I didn't really like the idea of looking daft in front of someone I knew. That's what strangers are for.

'So have you answered many more of these ads?' Molly asked.

'I had a massage,' I told her, as innocuously as I could, but it didn't work.

She burst out laughing just as she took a sip of her drink. 'What!'

'A massage,' I admitted. I sat down at the dining table and knew it was time to reveal all about my meeting with Lucy. I knew Molly would laugh at me, but it made sense to tell her what I had been up to. So I told her about seeing the advert and how terrified I was when I turned up at her house. I told her about standing in my turquoise boxer shorts and Lucy turning into a psychic. About turning up in my bowling shoes at yoga, saluting the sun, lying down like a corpse. And Pete, his videos and bedsit. I told her how bad I felt when I was in the taxi, being driven away from his house, his belongings on the back seat in bin bags.

Molly seemed interested, intrigued, and I was relieved she wasn't laughing any more. She wasn't making fun of me despite having every right to. It felt good to be unburdening myself of what I had been doing.

'There's just one thing I'm not sure about,' Molly told me.

'What's that?'

'Well, I think I understand what you're doing. Meeting these people sounds really interesting . . .' She hesitated as she worked out how to phrase the question. 'But what would you have done if Massage Lucy had been a prostitute?'

5

GERMAN LESSONS

It was Thursday evening, a week since I had been to yoga class. As James Lewis and the rest of the class were getting out their yoga mats and saluting the sun, I was at my dining table with a notebook. I didn't have time for yoga. I had a German lesson to prepare for.

The advert for German conversation classes had been in my favourite newsagent's window, Sears on Unthank Road, about a twenty-minute walk from my house. I emailed Leni, the girl who had posted the card in the window, and she replied to say she would be happy to meet me. I explained to her I had lived in both Germany and Austria and that although I was not fluent I would like to keep up my language skills. After exchanging a few emails we arranged to meet, so by way of preparation, I took out a book of German short stories and the massive German dictionary I hadn't touched since university, and settled down at the dining table to read for the rest of the evening, content at looking up any word I didn't know, finding a new thirst for knowledge. But unlike when I was doing my degree, when I sometimes wondered why I was putting myself through it all, this time I was really enjoying the process of learning German. When I was too tired to carry on reading I went to my room, but before I went to bed I tuned into an online Berlin radio station, and listened to it as I went to sleep, hoping vocab would seep in and I might dream in German.

The next morning I ate breakfast as I would have done living in Germany – bread, cheese, ham. I wanted to get in the right mood to meet Leni. I listened to the Berlin radio station again and really enjoyed the feeling it gave me, reigniting my passion for the country. I worked on year-long placements abroad twice – in Germany when I was twenty-one and in Vienna when I was twenty-four – and those had been some of the most enjoyable times of my life. I loved being there and one of the reasons I had arranged to meet Leni was because I'd always imagined I'd travel abroad again one day, maybe to live. Hamburg, Berlin, Munich were all places that I longed to go back to. I didn't want to feel like my time abroad had been wasted, that everything I had learned was going to be frittered away.

My German teacher at university said the best way to learn the language is to make sure your internal dialogue is all in German; whether walking down the street or in the supermarket all the thoughts running through your head should be in German rather than English. That way it should become second nature to switch from one language to the next. So as I walked to campus I spoke to myself in German, trying to get to grips with the lingo once more. I was meeting Leni at eleven o'clock at the University of East Anglia, where I had been a student. I set off and felt like I was on my way to an exam I hadn't prepared for. The flashbacks were inevitable: I walked past the house I lived in as a student; past the same chip shop; I crossed at the same set of traffic lights, cut through the forecourt of the same petrol station. I have good memories of university, but the closer I got, the more I realized that as time had passed I'd managed to forget the boring bits – the tedium of sitting through German lessons every day for three years and the tedium of having to do work for them every night. I think it's important to have a brain which glosses over the more dreary things in life and focuses on the positives, otherwise nobody would ever be able to get to sleep at night. Particularly those who studied for degrees in German.

In her emails Leni told me about herself – she was an Erasmus student, studying at UEA as part of her degree in English at university in Berlin. I decided that when we met I would try and greet her in German and explain that I wanted to speak as much German as possible. Our exchange of emails had been in English, but it seemed wrong to be using my mother tongue rather than hers. It's just that my German wasn't very good.

When I lived in Hanover teaching in a school, I spent most of my time with other English people, teaching assistants, students and expats, who all stuck together because we were embarrassed about our limited language skills. It was a vicious circle that meant we never really improved. I really regretted not ditching the English people and improving my German. That's why I went to have another go a couple of years later in Austria, again as a teaching assistant. I had learned from my mistakes, and made sure this time I didn't get too attached to any English people, and immersed myself in books written in German, often translations of English books I'd already read. Gradually I started to mix with locals, and occasionally allowed myself the treat of a glimpse at an English newspaper to look at the football scores. Despite this pledge, English was difficult to escape, particularly in a capital city in Europe, which is why speaking fluently always eluded me.

In more recent years potential linguists have had to have real dedication to learn a language, since English is everywhere. I was following in my mum's footsteps, who was a language assistant in France in the 1970s. I think that era would have suited me more, as there was no BBC website in those days, no email, no MTV. It was impossible to cheat. Any news came via letters written by friends and relatives who had made special journeys to queue at the post office and pay the correct postage. The Internet meant that even when I was in the middle of the Vienna Woods I was able to find out anything at the click of a button, and that made being abroad less special somehow; it is hard to integrate yourself within the local community when you have the world at your fingertips. That's the problem with the Internet, it means it's easy to retreat, to withdraw from life. Which is why I like the idea of newsagents' windows; it's some-where I feel that communities still exist.

I looked forward to meeting Leni. All people have their own preferences – some men prefer blonde girls, or tall girls, feisty girls or skinny girls. But my tastes have always been more European. I like my girls the same way I like my biscuits: German.

I arrived on campus an hour before the private tuition was due to begin, but milling around was one of my specialist subjects at UEA, so I managed to fill the time easily. I retraced my steps from my days as a student. I went to the office of my old teacher to say hello, tell him about my year in Vienna. He was happy to see me. One of life's pleasures is turning up somewhere unannounced and catching up with someone who has been a big part of your life. I told him about Vienna and that I was meeting Leni and he seemed impressed that I had made the most of what he'd taught me and continued to use it. Once we'd said goodbye I went for a quick pint of Grolsch in the university bar to help settle my nerves. The bar was empty. In a couple of weeks it would be freshers' week, a new intake of first years to start new lives as adults, to be homesick, cheat on their girlfriends and boyfriends, fall asleep in lecture theatres and have the best year of their life. I looked around the union bar and remembered my own first year at UEA and felt in equal measure jealous of those about to start their adventure, and relieved it was all behind me.

I made my way to the main entrance of the bar, where Leni and I had arranged to meet. As I stood waiting, I examined everyone that approached me, wondering if they were about to call out my name, introduce themselves and spend the next couple of hours talking to me in German. After waiting about ten minutes a girl looked optimistically in my direction.

'John?'

'Leni?'

We waved at each other in that pathetic way people do when they meet for the first time. Leni seemed friendly, with long brown hair and was dressed appropriately for the sunshine, in long flowing skirt, sunglasses and sandals.

'How are you?' she asked, beaming the kind of melting smile that has such force you re-evaluate your life. I sensed this was going to be an interesting afternoon. Straight away Leni seemed welcoming, but perhaps the evidence suggested that was always going to be the case – she had offered to teach German in her free time, she had arranged to meet me and had actually turned up.

'Should we sit down here?' she suggested, in English, pointing at the steps.

'Yeah, this is fine,' I said, replying in English, and we both made ourselves comfortable. The summer had spread out to mid-September, and other than a couple of overseas students, the university was practically deserted. Sitting on the steps in the sunshine brought back happy memories of when I was a wide-eyed fresh-faced student. The steps look miserable during the winter months, all sombre and grey with the rain, but when the sun shines students come out of nowhere and sprawl themselves across them and it becomes less an institute of education and more like the stone circle at Glastonbury. The gloomy concrete is soon hidden by a canvas of students with carrier bags of beer, packets of cigarettes and the whole afternoon ahead of them.

'Would you like a drink?' I asked Leni, again speaking in English, forgetting the pledge I had made to speak German, German, German. I was taking the easy option.

She nodded her head. 'Coca-Cola,' she replied, speaking the international language. I walked to the bar and ordered a Coke for her and another Grolsch for myself. I was going to need some help to get through this.

'So you lived in Vienna?' Leni asked, in German, as we sipped our drinks and disposed of the awkward preliminary small talk.

I nodded, which improved my German dramatically. And it stayed like this for a while: she fired questions, I struggled to grasp for an answer, my face blank. Despite my preparation over the previous twenty-four hours my German had not come back to me quickly. I stuttered and struggled to find any fluency. The natural shyness which had worried my primary school teachers so much when I would sit under the table playing with Unifix surfaced once again. I retreated into my shell too easily, but this time I was determined. I thought of Massage Lucy and tried to conduct myself with a positive attitude. I took a deep breath and started to speak in my best German.

I told Leni of the time I spent living in Hanover. I told her how I went ice skating on a frozen lake on my twenty-first birthday. As I told her these things, about the house, and the family I lived with and the places I had been, I remembered my year in Hanover with renewed clarity. It made me want to go back there, catch up with the friends I had spent time with. I wanted to see what the family I stayed with were doing, turn up unannounced in the school staffroom and find the teachers, thank them for all the help they had given me, and for making my year abroad more enjoyable than I had ever dared hope. It wasn't only my memory that was getting clearer; as I spoke it became easier to find the words I was looking for, I felt my accent sounding more natural, my intonation more precise, my lexicon more confident. Although that might have been the Grolsch.

Then I told Leni about Vienna. About living in the cottage in the Vienna Woods, my next-door neighbour who did my washing and ironing for me, and let me walk her dog once a week. I told her about Marie, and how upset I was when we broke up. As I spoke of these things I wondered whether I had been too hasty moving back to Norwich. The main reason I had contacted Leni was because I was getting increasingly involved with newsagents' windows, and she was another notch on the bedpost of people I had met that way, but it was doing me more good than I realized and put me in a contemplative mood.

Leni and I spent just under an hour sitting on the UEA steps. I felt slightly ashamed that my German was inadequate, but she had been very encouraging.

'I should give you your money,' I said, and handed across her fee of eight pounds. We'd made no agreement about how long our meeting would last, but I felt we had reached a natural conclusion, and I had started to run out of German words. Speaking in a foreign language is tiring and when I lived abroad I would regularly go to bed at eight o'clock in the evening, often when it was still daylight outside.

'Do you give many people tuition?' I asked Leni. She scrunched up her face and shook her head. 'Do you just advertise in that one newsagent's window?' I asked.

'And on the noticeboard at university,' she said.

'I hope more people reply,' I said, but knew that if they did so it was more likely to be through the noticeboard than the newsagent's window.

'It's been really useful,' I said, thanking her. 'If you want to do it again let me know,' I said, and she mimed typing on a keyboard and I promised myself I would email her in a few weeks and we would do this again.

'Do you want to stay for another drink?' I asked, but wasn't surprised when she said no. Already we were talking in English again, but this time I didn't feel guilty, I had done the hard work, I could afford to treat myself. I told Leni I'd be in touch and that perhaps we'd do it again one day, and I vowed to listen to more German radio, to read more German books and be able to talk to her much more fluently if we were to meet again. I went back to the bar to have another pint of Grolsch, because I felt I deserved it, and also because beer's really cheap in student bars.

6

THE BEAVER'S UNIFORM

Furnishing my house and buying Pete's videos had put me severely out of pocket, but despite this I wanted to know more about the people who wrote out these cards and tried to sell things and advertise services. There is a story behind every single card advertised, whether it's advertising an unused wedding dress or someone looking for their lost kitten. I really couldn't justify carrying on spending money, and I thought maybe my experiment with newsagents was over. But standing outside a shop one day, one advert out of a mosaic of cards intrigued me.

For sale, Beaver's uniform, £8.

After debating whether or not I should respond, I surrendered to my instinct and made the call. The opportunity to buy a Beaver's uniform was one I didn't want to turn down. While furnishing the house I had met fascinating people, listened to their stories and was relishing the chance to buy more things through newsagents, if for no other reason than to tell Molly about it. I had found a community I never knew existed; this was the heart of rural Britain and it was inviting me inside. I had learned that everyone has a story to tell, and that people who live very ordinary lives are much more fascinating than TV presenters or pop stars. People who write out these cards are inviting strangers into their homes, and curiosity was continually getting the better of me.

I dialled the number, and at first there was no answer, but like any good cold caller I persevered. My brashness and slightly inflated sense of self-esteem was due partly to the two glasses of red wine I had enjoyed while watching the lunchtime episode of *Neighbours*. This was the life I lived when I had a day off work. Then finally there was an answer. I spoke to a woman who said her name was Michelle and she told me her address, which was just ten minutes away. And so I arranged to go round later that afternoon to buy her son's Beaver uniform, poised to waste my money once again.

I was a Cub when I was little and thought that Beavers were something similar, but I wasn't exactly sure what kind of organization it was, whether for boys or girls and what age a Beaver would be. I felt I should find these things out, in case I was asked the not unreasonable question of why a twenty-six-year-old man would want to buy the uniform of a small child. I was on shaky ground, and telling the truth was probably my best option. I knew this, but decided that a cover story would be less embarrassing than saying I was buying random things from newsagents' windows. I whirred up my laptop and went online to create a plausible alibi. I was about to type 'Beavers' into an Internet search engine, but realized this would come up with some unsavoury sites, so I refined my search to 'Beavers' Uniforms'. This gave me all the information I needed to know, that Beavers were for both boys and girls, aged six to eight. Quickly I was able to create a story which developed thus: I had a five-year-old cousin – a boy – who was going to start Beavers in a few weeks and we needed a uniform for him. If Michelle asked anything slightly complicated, or began using Beaver terminology that confused me I would plead ignorance, explain that I was just collecting the jumper on behalf of my auntie, who was busy with a house full of toddlers, at which the Beaver's mum would tut in sympathy and say 'Tell me about it.'

I was pretty nervous when I walked to the Beaver's house. It was a street I had walked down hundreds of times before, but never with such caution. I was a bit worried the police would become involved. As I neared the house, the sky turned dark, the wind picked up and it started to rain quite heavily. I directed a Sid James-style wink towards pathetic fallacy and looked for number 94.

I hate houses with no doorbells. I knocked with a firm rat-a-tat and a woman I assumed to be Michelle answered. She wore a bright-red cardigan and was in her early thirties, slim with long black hair in a ponytail. Her chattiness put me at ease. She was cheerful and welcoming, as I had expected after our conversation on the phone earlier. I apologized for being wet but the *bloody weather* platitudes allowed for a smooth transition from being a stranger on a doorstep to sitting in an armchair as Michelle went through to the kitchen.

'He only went to Beavers twice,' she told me, referring to her off-screen son as she came back into the front room with a towel for me to dry my hair. 'But then he gave up. He didn't really like it very much.'

I felt a bit jealous of the Beaver – if it had been my mum I would have been forced to keep on turning up until I'd had my money's worth out of the jumper, no matter how unhappy being a Beaver made me. I would never have joined a group and then been allowed to quit two weeks later. Kids have it so easy today. My hair tousled, I gave Michelle her towel back; she took it through to the kitchen and came back in with the Beaver's jumper and a yellow and red neckerchief.

'I'm really sorry for my bad effort at ironing!' she said with an embarrassed smile. Perhaps she assumed it was the creases that were making me feel uncomfortable rather than the absurdity of the situation I had put myself in. 'Ironing isn't my strong point. Or housework!' she said as she looked around the room at the clutter of toys, open DVD cases and washing baskets of dirty clothes. 'Or cooking,' she continued, ruefully. 'Also,' she said, showing me the label sticking out of the jumper, 'I hope it isn't a problem, John, but I've written his name in biro.' Michelle looked at me like she thought forgiveness might be out of the question.

'It was just too sociable for him,' she told me. 'There was too much interaction. He's only really happy when he's here, at home with us. But we're trying to discourage that, get him out of his shell.'

'I was the same when I was little,' I told her, thinking of sitting by myself at Cubs, changing by myself after swimming lessons.

'He just refuses to join in with the other children,' Michelle continued. 'It was the same at other groups we've tried to get him to join. He just didn't make friends at drama club, he stood by himself at football.' Michelle wiped a wisp of hair from her eye. I imagine her concern was similar to that of my mum and dad when I reluctantly edged my way out of the door to go to school every morning, knowing I'd be standing on my own in the playground.

'I think that's completely normal,' I told her, not knowing whether it was my role to reassure Michelle or just give her the money for the uniform and get on my way. 'Some kids are just shy.'

'He's starting karate next month,' she told me, and smiled. 'That might be more suitable. He'll probably enjoy kicking someone in the goolies.'

'Who wouldn't?' I replied, and hoped I wouldn't be seeing a karate kit advertised on a card in a newsagent's window a few months later. I couldn't afford to buy that too.

'Is it the right size?' Michelle asked, holding the jumper up, a sleeve in each hand. This was it, this was my get-out clause, my route back to normality. It would have been perfectly plausible to simply apologize, tell her the jumper was far too small and leave it at that. After all the Beaver I was buying the uniform for was entirely of my own invention, he could be any size I wanted him to be. I could have just told her that my Beaver was a bit bigger than her Beaver and I'd have been able to walk out without having to pay any of my hard-earned money. But I felt I couldn't just leave it at that, I wanted more. It wasn't enough to simply be welcomed inside Michelle's house, I felt I was there to help her out, just as with Pete and his videos. I felt there was a connection between this shy boy, and me, an overgrown shy boy. I had grown attached, and felt it was right to seal the deal.

'Yeah, it'll fit perfectly,' I told her, holding the jumper in my hands, barely bigger than a handkerchief. It wasn't just the Beaver I felt sympathy for, I really liked Michelle. She clearly found things a bit of a struggle sometimes, with her ironing and cooking and decision-making. Perhaps she should have allowed her son the time to decide whether or not he liked going to Beavers before she bought a uniform for him, and she certainly should have waited a couple of weeks before she biroed his name on the label. I knew that I could have knocked a couple of pounds off the price because she had written the name on the label, but I sensed that I'd just go 'OK' when she suggested a sum. I don't have it in my nature to be ruthless. Sometimes kids are just shy.

'Who's the jumper for?' Michelle asked. 'Boy or girl?'

'A boy,' I replied, not even needing to lie. I just didn't explain that the boy was me. 'How much is it?' I asked.

'Eight pounds,' she said, almost like an apology. We were far from budding entrepreneurs. People like me and Michelle would be much happier in life if you could use fish fingers and cuddles as currency. I jingled pound coins in my pocket.

'Had the advert been up a long time?' I asked, as I handed her the money.

'Yeah, quite a long time. Maybe ten weeks.'

'Just as well I came along!' I said, and she nodded. The way she smiled as she curled her fingers around the pound coins justified the money I had spent. We said our goodbyes, my job there was done.

It seemed a shame it had taken so long to find someone interested in the uniform. The fact that the card for it had been up
in the newsagent's window for ten weeks meant that Michelle's
profit margins had been dented – at 25p a week ten weeks
would have cost her £2.50. And some newsagents charged
more, some 30p, one fat cat shopkeeper even charged £1! That's
London prices. Selling things through newsagents' windows
didn't seem a very efficient way of making money.

At least the whole transaction had turned out to be relatively
straightforward, I hadn't needed to worry about a cover story.
Michelle did not question the fact that I looked too young to
father a Beaver. Which was a fact I did not consider until I was
walking away, when it dawned on me that there were people
my age with Beavers, Cubs, Brownies, taking their children to
the leisure centre to teach them how to swim, swinging them
round by their ankles in the garden, going to sports day and
parents' evenings. Two of my friends from school had recently
had babies, and they were younger than me. So clearly I was
old enough to have a Beaver of my own, yet instead had no
money, just a Beaver's uniform, a second-hand single bed and a
job on minimum wage.

Once I had left Michelle's house I started to wonder what I
was going to do with a Beaver's uniform. Would I be prepared
to sell it at a loss? I couldn't cope with the idea of waiting for ten
weeks on the off-chance my phone would ring and someone
would tell me they were interested in buying it. I walked back
home, confused about what I had done, when I heard a voice
call out my name.

'John!'

I panicked, and looked around. It was Stewart, one of my best friends from university. I hadn't seem him since I'd been back in Norwich, and these weren't exactly the ideal conditions for meeting again. I really hoped he wouldn't ask what was in the bag.

'I heard you were back in town. How's your new house?' he asked.

'Really good. You should come round.' I was terrified he would ask me what was in the bag. There was no way I could explain why I had a Beaver's uniform.

'Yeah, I will do. How was Vienna?' he asked, and I tried to sum up my year in a minute, and in turn asked what he was doing, the whole time knowing I had a Beaver's uniform in a plastic bag.

I hadn't needed to panic; Stewart didn't seem suspicious, and we said goodbye and carried on in our intended directions. I upped my pace, desperate to get back home, taking strides a triple-jumper would have been proud of. Once I made it inside I breathlessly double-locked the front door behind me and peered through the spyhole to make sure I hadn't been fol-lowed. I wrapped the Beaver's uniform in several layers of carrier bags, which I zipped up inside a rucksack and hid under my bed. Surely it would be safe in there. I couldn't justify what I had just done. Meeting Stewart was a heart-stopping moment where my newsagent's window life came perilously close to meeting my everyday Norwich life and it made me feel uncomfortable. Already I hated owning the Beaver's uniform. I wasn't even sure whether it was the sort of thing I could tell Molly. She had thought going to see a woman who might be a prostitute was quite out of character.

We still didn't really know each other that well, and this could prompt her to completely re-evaluate her views of me. I didn't want her to think I was crazy and end up moving out. My only option was to try to forget about the Beaver's uniform completely, out of sight, out of mind. I just prayed that nothing happened to me, that I wasn't involved in a pile-up on the A13, or in a skydiving accident, or carbon monoxide poisoning – anything that would put my parents in the position where they had to clear out my room, where grief would turn to confusion as they found a Beaver's uniform under my bed.

I thought about Michelle a lot over the next couple of weeks, not just the pathos of the unwanted jumper, but about what she had said about her lack of success with newsagents' windows. Dan who sold me the beds had experienced similar problems, as had Leni when it came to advertising private tuition. I wondered why it was. Hundreds of people must have looked in the window at the Beaver's uniform advert, yet no one replied. These adverts are read every day; I've seen lots of people stop and browse. They are discreet and unassuming, rooted in the subconscious of the local community. But although many people look at news-agents' windows, clearly there are few who actually reply. Except for me, that is. It seemed I was single-handedly keeping it all afloat.

I felt sympathetic towards Michelle, and was glad I'd met her. It made me determined to meet more people in the same way. What had initially started as a way to furnish my new house had turned into something on a much bigger scale. I had only met a few people through newsagents' windows but Michelle, Massage Lucy, and Donna and Mike had given me the sense that I was part of a community I had never been aware of. These people seemed honest and friendly and were working hard, living very ordinary lives. Perhaps they did not have much cash or were fighting a constant battle against modern life, and I was happy to give them my money without getting a lot back in return. I was having a surprising amount of fun. If I had my own way I would never go to a shop again, I'd buy everything in other people's living rooms. So I decided to try and meet more people who used newsagents' windows, and find out more about the community in which they existed.

7

THE BLOOD DONOR

'You've got lovely eyes,' my nurse Debi told me as I reclined on the bed, my left sleeve rolled up. 'Big and blue,' she continued. 'I could gaze into them all day.'

I knew that Debi was just doing her job and distracting me from the needle she was about to jab in my arm, but I'll always accept a compliment about my eyes in exchange for pain. I can't imagine that anyone wouldn't. Molly had agreed to come with me to the school hall to give blood. She had done it a few times before, whereas this was my first, and she promised me it would be OK. I was sceptical.

Practically every newsagent's window in Norwich advertises blood donation sessions. It became apparent that giving blood was a duty I couldn't really avoid, in fact *shouldn't* really avoid. Which is why I decided to find out what it was like to have a needle plunged in my arm.

Our appointments were at Norwich High School for Girls. We followed the bright-red *Blood* signs which led us into the hall, but it resembled no school hall I had ever seen. It was like a war zone, with nurses tending to patients on operating beds, the walking wounded queuing by a vat of boiling water for weak tea in polystyrene cups. Everywhere I looked there were men and women covered in bandages. Well, perhaps nothing as extreme as bandages, but a couple of people had plasters on their fingers. The lack of privacy took me by surprise, us *good people* were given no privacy while we were selflessly doing our *good deeds*; we had no curtain to draw, no screen, no special little room in which to compose ourselves for what was about to happen.

'I'm Trish,' a nurse wearing blue NHS polyester said to me. 'I'll be your donor carer. How are you feeling?'

'I'm fine,' I told her but it wasn't the truth. I was feeling a bit light-headed and wanted to go home. Trish gave us forms to fill in and a folder new doners needed to look through to become acquainted with the process. This was where it started to go wrong. As soon as I started to read I felt even more queasy; the word *vein* leaped out at me from the page like a burst ventricle. It left me feeling dizzy, so much so I thought I was going to have to run out of the room. What I had been trying to avoid had sunk in – that despite all the niceties and platitudes from the staff I was going to be stabbed with a needle and crippled with pain. I wasn't sure I could go through with it. I contemplated locking myself in the toilet, or running away, keeping my blood in my own arm.

I didn't expect that reading about the procedure would make me react this way. I was a wreck. There are certain words that cause people to shudder, turn their legs to jelly, and for me these are needle, vein, cyst and endoscope. It's at times like these I realize I am nothing more than a cowardly, terrified wimp who can't deal with discomfort. I have an occasional misplaced belief that I am tough and cool but I'm not. I like Richard Curtis films. I always hope it snows at Christmas. I cried a bit when Monica and Chandler got married in *Friends*. I really wanted to sit down cross-legged, bang the floor with my fists and wail at the top of my voice.

'It's fine, stop overreacting. It's just giving a bit of blood,' Molly reassured me, looking up from her magazine. But I couldn't escape. I had already told my mum and dad what I was doing that afternoon. I'd told my sister. I had sent out telegrams to long-lost friends, distant members of my family I'd never met. I'd taken out a full-page advert in all the broadsheets so that as many people as possible would be made aware of what a good person I was being by giving blood. Word would probably reach Buckingham Palace and Downing Street; they would be engraving my name on medals. There was no way of getting out of the fact that in an hour's time I was going to be holding a piece of cotton wool to my arm, and weigh a pint less than I had that morning.

'Yeah, I'll be fine,' I said, more to myself than to Molly. I closed the folder and handed it back to the nurse. I decided to remain seated and accept what was coming to me; people had survived worse than this in the past. I looked around. There were four beds in the school hall, all occupied by people attached to tubing. The waiting area was full of people eager to take their place, doing it out of nothing but kindness. We were doing it because hospitals continually need fresh supplies of blood. The National Blood Service is integral to saving people's lives every day. Those who volunteer to give blood are doing something very special. Every year in the UK over a million people donate blood, and this is used not only in life-saving transfusions but also in improving the quality of life for patients who have various illness or are recuperating from operations. But a million people is still only a tiny fraction of the population, and although the efforts of those attending places such as Norwich High School for Girls, who have registered as donors, are hugely admirable and the generosity is staggering, sadly it still does not provide the levels needed to satisfy the requirements of the National Health Service. It is through advertising in places such as newsagents' windows that people are recruited, and everyone waiting alongside me was helping the life expectancy of strangers, and in doing so reserving a room with a view in Heaven, or at least an en suite in limbo. Working at the reception desk in a hotel it's easy to believe the world is full of estate agents and nobheads but the more people I was meeting, the more I trusted the world. There were more nice people than the *Daily Mail* would lead you to believe. Everyone sitting in the waiting room, or lying on beds giving blood, revealed that sometimes people just do good deeds; it's nice to be nice.

Soon Molly and I were separated, and I was taken away by my donor carer. Trish pricked my index finger to test the iron in my blood, to detect any antibodies or viruses in my bloodstream, any problem that would mean I wouldn't be able to donate. Apparently cowardice isn't a good enough reason. Trish covered the speck of blood on my finger with a dab of cotton wool.

'Are you allergic to plasters?'

'No,' I said as she unwrapped an Elastoplast from its packet. 'I'm allergic to cats though.' Sometimes when I'm scared about something I try too hard to appear relaxed.

'Your blood is fine, very healthy,' she told me after a couple of minutes. 'Take a seat. If you have any questions I'll be here.' Trish directed me to a second waiting area, full of contented people wearing nice jumpers. I was amazed that my blood was OK to use. 'Very healthy.' It seemed absurd. I was fully expecting to fall at the first hurdle, that my blood would have been inadequate somehow, meaning I would be able to go home with a legitimate excuse. But it was fine – maybe I am a normal functioning human being after all.

I sat and stared at the floor contemplating what was about to happen when a man sitting next to me stood up to call across to another man who had just arrived.

'Hello there!' he called out, and the two warmly shook hands, excited at bumping into each other.

'We have to stop meeting like this!' the other said, and they both sat down either side of me, not saying anything else, but their presence relaxed me. It can't be too horrific if people keep coming back, giving their blood away like it grows on trees.

'John Osborne,' a nurse called, and Debi gazed into my deep-blue eyes as she told me to make myself comfortable, which would have been easier if she hadn't been attaching tubes and piping to my arm.

'This is your first time,' she said, as a statement rather than a question, and I realized my bluff of acting tough had failed. 'It's good of you to do this,' she said, and I tried to shrug it off, suggesting I have good deeds pouring through my very healthy red blood cells. Debi wrapped a cuff around the bicep on my left upper arm and squeezed a valve, strangulating the blood flow.

'You need to wiggle your fingers. Open and close your hand,

let the blood flow while I try and find the best vein we can use,' she told me, running two fingers up and down my arm as I wiggled my digits like my life depended on it, and I realized needle time was imminent.

'Ah-ha,' she said. 'Found one, this will do nicely. OK, we're going to take around four hundred and seventy millilitres of blood.' The world has gone metric since the days of *Hancock's Half Hour.*

'This is the worst bit,' she told me, then a split second later she jabbed me and I looked away and closed my eyes tightly but there wasn't really any pain. But so much of this kind of situation is psychosomatic; the anticipation of needles is much worse than the actual pinprick, and those who feel faint and queasy do so more at the sight of a needle and the thought of it sticking into their arm than the pain, which in most cases, such as giving blood, is only very slight.

'The whole process takes about seven minutes,' Debi told me as my blood started to decant. 'I'll leave you alone for now but I'll be back to check up on you. If you need anything just scream!'

I didn't dare look to my left, I didn't want to see blood oozing out of my arm, swishing and swirling through tubes and dribbling into a bag. Instead I looked to my right, where there was the much more palatable sight of the good people of Norwich, sitting patiently, waiting for their turn to take my place. I assumed I was a bit of a role model to them, that they were all looking at me and thinking: 'My God he's heroic. What a guy. I bet he's got brilliant haemoglobin. Look at his big blue eyes. I could gaze into them all day.'

I felt that giving blood would be a rare chance for me to do a good deed in what sometimes felt like an unproductive life I led. I carried the odd suitcase for businessmen but only in the hope that I'd get a tip, and also because I'd get told off if I didn't. But this was different. I liked the feeling of being one of the good guys, contributing something to society in time I would otherwise have been at home. In everyday life you are unlikely to have the opportunity to dive in front of a bullet for a loved one, to piggyback orphans from a burning building, or scoop a child into your arms on a busy street as a lorry screeches, swerves, onlookers gasp and a mother says to you 'I don't know how I can ever . . .' as you walk away, pretending you don't hear offers of rewards. But heroism isn't reserved for Hollywood romcoms, it is as achievable as spending an hour of your day giving blood. I thought of the woman who told me I'd dropped a fiver on the floor outside the yoga class. She could have kept it herself, spent it on sweets. That's what I would have done. But the world isn't full of estate agents and nobheads. As I sat in the waiting room I thought about a story my sister had told me recently.

Her boyfriend had seen a sign on a gate at the end of someone's drive saying *To whoever stole my children's bicycles, thank you for ruining our Christmas.*

He was moving house and took out all the old cuddly toys he'd had since he was little from under his bed. He put them all in a box, went round to the house and left them on the doorstep. He wrote a note and put it on the gate saying: *To the children who had their bicycles stolen, I hope this helps make things better.*

A few days later he walked past the house again and saw a third note, saying *To whoever left toys for my children, thank you for restoring my faith in humanity.*

'Blimey,' Debi said, returning to my bed, inspecting the outflow, 'it's really gushing out.' I couldn't feel any gushing sensation, and felt uncomfortable having a startled nurse at my bedside. Typical, my first go at giving blood and I haemorrhage. I was going to die in Norwich High School for Girls. This isn't how things were supposed to turn out for me. 'You're doing really well,' Debi said to me, a broad smile on her face as she left me to gush and frantically wiggle my fingers while I wondered whether I was going to live or die. Two minutes later she returned and unplugged me.

'Right, all done,' she said. I opened my eyes, sat upright and held cotton wool against my arm until she had covered the precious area with a plaster, which I would wear like a badge of honour. 'You can stay on the bed until you feel comfortable, and then help yourself to orange squash and biscuits from Mary.'

I stayed on the bed long enough for Debi to walk away and check on another patient, but I didn't want to spend any more time sitting around. I wanted to get on with my day. Recuperating is for wimps. I was too rock and roll to sit on a bed. I was ready for my orange squash.

'Would you like to book your next appointment?' Mary, the nurse in charge of snacks, asked as I sipped Kia Ora and nibbled a Jammie Dodger. I nodded, she opened up the diary and I booked another appointment. You are only allowed to give blood every four months, otherwise I'd have been back there the next day, striding in confidently, my shirtsleeve already rolled up, ready for more needles and cotton wool. I drank my squash as I waited for Molly, who I could see was just rolling her sleeve back down, chatting animatedly to one of the nurses. As I waited I wondered what was happening to the blood we had donated. I imagined it tearing down the motorway in the back of a truck heading to the labs. I felt that my blood would definitely save someone's life. Maybe it would even be a celebrity. I wondered whether there was a box I could have ticked to make sure my blood would definitely be given to someone who's been on telly.

'How do you feel?' Molly asked when she joined me afterwards.

'Really good,' I said, and we walked away from the high school, me with my head held high, full of pride and by the time we got back home I still didn't feel even remotely woozy. It didn't even hurt when I took the plaster off in the shower.

8

THE BIKE

It was 6 a.m. I left the house and started the long walk to the hotel. I looked in the newsagent's window I passed en route. So far this window had been fruitless; it was the most barren newsagent's window in the county, with only two cards, both with faded handwriting verging on the invisible; one advertising Doberman puppies, which were surely fully grown by now, the other the ubiquitous Man with a Van 'for all your removal needs', who had probably since retired. As I approached the newsagent's I noticed a new set of adverts had been placed. Brand-new things were available for me, offering fresh opportunities, enticing me to spend more money. It was as exciting as getting the Christmas Argos catalogue when I was little, flicking to the back and looking at the toys.

Immediately there was something I wanted to buy – a bike. It was advertised at £45, in perfect condition, hardly used. The more I thought about it the more I realized how much I needed this bike. Walking to work was a couple of miles in each direction, I hadn't foreseen how time-consuming it would be when I took the job. This would speed my mornings up, meaning I could spend more time under my duvet before an early start. A bicycle would certainly be more use than a Beaver's uniform – an idiom I feared would catch on if I ever told any of my friends what I had been doing. I wrote down the phone number and waited until it was a reasonable time to make the call. Some people don't like being telephoned at six in the morning.

I decided 10 a.m. was a legitimate time to call, and excused myself from the reception desk while I went outside to dial the number. I paced up and down on the forecourt by the hotel entrance. The phone was ringing, I waited for a 'hello', and was about to give up when, once again, I was making arrangements with a stranger.

'I only put it up last night!' he said, genuinely excited. 'I didn't think anyone would call this quickly!'

The bike was mine. Considering Michelle's lack of response with the Beaver's uniform it seemed reasonable for him to have such low expectations. This guy was just lucky to have caught the attention of the most keen user of newsagents' windows Norwich had ever known. I went back to work and spent the rest of my shift carrying suitcases for businessmen, hoping the time would pass with as few problems as possible, slightly resenting anybody who had the cheek to check in to my hotel as I waited for the clock to turn, picturing myself doing wheelies down a hill.

The bike man said I was welcome to go round at any time after seven that evening, which meant after work I had time to go home and eat (healthily) before I went round to strike a deal. He gave me precise directions to his house; he lived in a part of

Norwich I wasn't really familiar with, which gave me the opportunity to find out what would happen if I turned left at the bottom of my road rather than my customary right.

It was a beautiful Norwich evening, Norfolk has fantastic sunsets, and it was a nice evening to spend walking, watching the sun gradually dip until it disappeared completely. This was just as well, as judging by my A–Z I had a long way to go. The journey was made even longer by my inability to navigate side streets and an overcomplicated numbering system on the road the bike man lived on. Clearly numerical order had been eschewed in favour of a more scattered approach. By the time I had found the right place dusk was turning into night-time. I walked through an alleyway and at the bottom of a set of metal steps was a grey-haired man, smoking a roll-up. His presence startled me a little.

'Are you number twenty-one?' I asked.

'Yes,' he said with an *I've been expecting you* laugh. He was a wafer-thin man in his sixties with pipe-cleaner arms and legs and a beautiful, handsome smile. 'You've come for the bike?' he asked.

I nodded.

He gestured at a cat on his doorstep, curled up in a ball.

'It's because of her that I have to sell it.' The cat looked down at the floor, prompting the bike man to lower his voice. 'She's on her way out,' he whispered. He shook his head, clearly upset at having to say the words. 'It costs me thirty-five pounds just to get her seen by the vet,' he said, dropping his cigarette butt to the floor and rummaging around in his pockets before producing a bunch of keys. 'And that's before you add on the costs of treatment.' He walked over to the shed. 'Spend all my life in that bloody vet's, sending me bankrupt!' He laughed and went over to stroke the cat.

'The bike's in pretty good condition,' he told me, putting one of the keys jangling on the ring into the shed's padlock. He wheeled the bike over to me. He walked with a pronounced limp, his left leg propelled almost at a right angle, and clearly he realized I'd noticed the unusual way he walked.

'I've got a pin in my leg from a motorcycle accident in the Sixties,' he told me, his voice reedy, and I sensed that even speaking caused pain. 'She's no better,' he said, gesturing towards his cat. 'I saw her walking the other day, one paw fine, the other front paw badly injured. I looked at her and said, "You're taking the piss out of me, aren't you?!"' He spluttered a cough which was half wheeze, half chuckle, and presented the bike to me, like Santa with bronchitis. It was shiny blue, and looked like it had barely been used. I had been trying to maintain the healthy lifestyle Massage Lucy had recommended to me. Twice a week I went swimming in the hotel pool, I was drinking water where once I'd have downed Pepsi, ate soup where I'd have once wolfed down a thin and crispy pepperoni. On one trip to a supermarket I looked at the conveyor belt and it looked like the shopping of someone I had never met before – Sicilian orange juice, asparagus, a mango.

I sat on the saddle to test it for size. I rode around the back-yard, down the alleyway, turned round and came back.

'It's great,' I said. It had been a long time since I had ridden a bike that worked – the bike I had last owned was the one I'd used for my paper round as a thirteen-year-old, and it had been falling apart. It had no brakes, which meant I had to develop my own method of coming to a stop, which generally involved brick walls or hedges. If anyone encroached on the pavement in the direction I was heading I had to shout at them to get out of the way. Eventually the bike was stolen when I locked it up at university. When I came back from my German seminar and saw the railing where my bike had once been it had really upset me, but in hindsight it could have saved my life. Norwich like all cities has a big problem with people nicking bikes, and now that I'd met this man and his poorly cat I really hoped the thieves would spare me with this one.

'You're much taller than me,' my new business associate observed. 'I can raise the saddle for you if you like?'

I hesitated, not wanting to put him to any trouble, but couldn't ignore that there was a height difference of perhaps a foot between us and it would have been useful to raise the saddle a little.

'If that's OK?' I asked, grateful for the help. I am hopeless with anything to do with spanners, hammers or screwdrivers. He took out another key from his bunch and walked over to a second shed which he opened up, took out an Allen key and awkwardly staggered back to me and the bike. He twisted the bolt on the saddle and asked me to straddle my leg over to check it was set at the correct height for me to cycle comfortably. When he was finished, the cat and I watched as he padlocked both sheds again.

'So how much did I advertise it for?' he asked. 'We agreed on five hundred and ninety-nine pounds, didn't we?'

He wheezed another chuckle while rolling another cigarette.

I was reassured by his kindness, he was easily the nicest person I had met in a long time, even by the high standard set by those associated with newsagents' windows.

'The advert I saw said forty-five pounds,' I told him, although if I'd had five hundred and ninety-nine in my pocket I'd have handed it over gladly, wanting to help this man as much as I could.

'That's right,' he said, still chuckling at his own joke. There was no way I was going to go home without this bike. I looked forward to cycling to work, into town, everywhere I went I would take it with me. I took the money out of my pocket. Just like with the video collection and the Beaver's uniform I felt this was no time to negotiate, especially after he had gone to the effort of opening both the sheds and adjusting the seat, clearly in discomfort as he was doing so. I liked this man, I wanted him to have my money, him and his cat needed it more than I did. I would only waste it on avocados and fruit juice. I was aware that yet again I was running scared of knocking the price down; Massage Lucy would be ashamed of me. She would want me to stick up for myself, to make sure I got as good a deal as possible, not to be too concerned about other people's feelings. And that's what I wanted too, I wanted to be a ruthless businessman, like Richard Branson, Alan Sugar, Mike Baldwin. But I was more interested in meeting people than getting good value for money. I handed over my wad of five-pound notes.

'Thank you,' he said to me with a smile, enjoying the weight of the notes in his hand. He put the money in the pocket of his jeans, ready to be handed over at the vet's the next day.

'It's a really good bike,' I told him, grabbing hold of the handlebars, which he held out for me to take. I checked the brakes, looked at the gear cogs. Not a hint of rust, not a squeak to be heard.

'What's your name?' I asked as I prepared to cycle away.

'John,' he told me.

'I'm John too,' I said.

'Johns everywhere!' he said, laughing again, which this time culminated in a full-blown wheeze attack that had him bent double. 'Stick to the pavement!' he shouted out to me once he got his breath back. 'It's dangerous having bicycles on the road. If you hit a car, I'm not responsible!' he warned, wheezing out his laugh once more as the evening darkened over our heads. He waved to gesture that he was OK, so I wheeled my new bike down the pathway and John took out his packet of tobacco and rolled another cigarette, licking the Rizla. I looked forward to having a bicycle again and hoped the money I'd spent on it would make a difference to John and his cat.

'Johns everywhere,' I said to myself, and rode on the pavement, because that's what he had told me to do. I was red in the face with the effort of pedalling up a hill, but as soon as I was at the top of it I was able to speed down, faster and faster, no hands, faster and faster, then skidded to a stop at the top of my drive. Life was starting to seem easier.

9

TAYLOR'S NEWS

I was at my friend Stewart's house. After seeing him the day I bought the Beaver's uniform I wanted to meet up with him, catch up in more sedate surroundings. He was one of the first friends I made when I started university, and we were housemates for two years. After graduating, he had stayed in Norwich, and followed the familiar route of well-paid job, car, girlfriend and mortgage, which was favoured by so many of those I knew. We didn't really share the same group of friends any more, people we used to hang around with at university had moved away from the area, but I still went round to his house sometimes because we both liked listening to Bob Dylan and watching football. I think having anything more than that in a friendship is just showing off.

'You know Taylor's News?' Stewart said to me. I nodded, but the question was rhetorical, the newsagent's was across the road from the house we used to live in and we'd been in there most days for two years for *Viz* magazine or Hula Hoops.

'Did you know the man who works there used to play for West Ham?'

'Really?'

'Yeah, Alan Taylor. He was on the news yesterday; it looks like he was pretty good, too.'

Stewart had no idea I had such an obsession with newsagents. I was reluctant to tell anyone other than Molly so there was no way he could have known the reasons I was the owner of a bicycle, bathroom scales and a man's entire video collection. The only reason he told me about Alan Taylor was that going to that newsagent was such a shared experience for us, we always liked the nice man behind the counter. Every time we went in there, no matter what time it was, the same white-haired, tall, thin man would always be stood at the till. He didn't seem to mind whether we were thumbing through every page of every magazine or were buying milk at 6 a.m., he would be nothing but cordial, friendly and jolly, surely the most important character-istics in a newsagent's armoury.

In 1975 West Ham United won the FA Cup, beating Fulham 2–0, and both goals were scored by Alan Taylor. He signed for the club on his twenty-first birthday, and shortly afterwards he played in the final at Wembley, sharing the same turf as such football legends as Bobby Moore and Trevor Brooking. Later in his career he left West Ham to join Norwich City, and when he retired years later he opened up Taylor's News.

It's strange to think of a retired footballer setting his alarm for five o'clock every morning to insert supplements into broad-sheets after spending most of his life practising scoring headers from corners and playing in front of thousands of people, the crowd cheering when he scored. It's difficult to imagine a retired Wayne Rooney stood behind the counter selling the *Norwich*

Evening News and packets of Benson & Hedges, or David Beckham telling off paperboys for cycling across a customer's front lawn. In fact these days it's hard to imagine anyone opening a newsagent's, footballer or not. The more time I spent reading about news-agents the more I realized what a gruelling business people like Alan Taylor were faced with. Newspapers are printed every single day of the year with the exception of Christmas Day, which means opening up seven days a week, 364 days a year. And newsagents are a major target for crime, vulnerable as they tend to handle cash rather than credit cards. Any robber can simply walk in with a baseball bat, there is little line of defence. Being a newsagent doesn't seem an appealing career choice in the twenty-first century. Not only are people shopping at supermarkets, where everything is all under the same roof, but also more and more people get their information online, and that trend is going to continue; newspapers are in decline as much as the stores that sell them.

In a stressful time for small businesses, owning a newsagent's seemed like hard work for not much reward. Since I had started looking in newsagents' windows I had noticed three newsagents in Norwich had gone out of business, the *Open* sign had been flipped to *Closed* for one final time, the shutters pulled down. Perhaps this was natural attrition, that the owners were now happily retired. That's more palatable than the thought of a newsagent looking at his bills, tapping at a calculator, not being able to sleep at night. Gradually the concept of the newsagent is becoming an increasingly old-fashioned one, as quaint as the milkman clinking bottles on your doorstep.

Over the next few weeks I tried to find out more about the

life of a newsagent – the role they play in the community, and whether it was really worth all the early mornings. And I was surprised as I gradually found out it wasn't quite the bleak picture that I had built it up to be.

One newsagent, who looked like Godfrey in *Dad's Army*, told me the main problems newsagents have had to deal with.

'The way people buy their dailies and weeklies has changed,' he explained, his accent as Norfolk as Colman's mustard. 'In the early Nineties only a few supermarkets sold newspapers and magazines, now all of them do.' As we spoke a couple of boys and a girl came in, fluorescent bags over their shoulders, taking stacks of bound papers and waving goodbye to the newsagent, the door dinging every time it opened and closed. It brought back happy memories of when I did the same, for a little paper shop near my house when I was young. 'There was a change in the law in 1994,' he continued, as I tried not to become too nostalgic, 'which meant anywhere that wanted to sell newspapers had the right to do so, like Starbucks and Marks & Spencer. Prior to that, stores could only sell newspapers if they were given special clearance from news wholesalers that it would not infringe on existing newsagents. We were protected, but now, with increased competition, newsagents are closing down.'

'Do you think supermarkets will be the ruin of you?' I asked. Private Godfrey shook his head.

'We provide a personal service that supermarkets can't compete with. They will never have that personal touch. I know the brand of cigarette every customer smokes. I know the patterns and purchases of local people who shop here. I stand behind this counter all day, every day. No one buys anything without me knowing about it,' he said, smiling knowingly. 'Supermarkets will never be able to offer anything similar; with their turnover of staff and higher amount of customers, it makes it difficult to be on first-name terms. And even if they do get to know people's names they can't really afford to stop and have a chat. Not in the way I do. We're going to be fine here,' he assured me. 'Another thing worth noting is that although all supermarkets slash prices on many products, newspapers and magazines always cost the same. There are newsagents in danger though,' he admitted. 'We can't just roll with the punches, any business that just sits down and takes what is coming to them is in big, big trouble. We have had to diversify, encourage loyalty and new customers. It's tough, but not impossible.'

This made me feel much more positive about newsagents, so much so that it felt like there was no way supermarkets could survive, that it was them in danger of becoming extinct.

'So now I am far more flexible with store credit than I used to be,' he continued. 'I let my customers pay their bills whenever it's convenient to them. If you hassle them they won't come back. If they've had a bad month then I let them off, I know I'll get the money eventually. People are loyal to me, they've been coming to me for years; it's the way it's always been.'

'And what will happen when you retire?' I asked. The newsagent chuckled, and I sensed it was time to make a move.

Back at home I went online to check whether everything Stewart had told me about Alan Taylor was true. Once I'd read about his goal-scoring exploits I carried on looking up other stories about newsagents.

I read about a card that had been placed in a newsagent's window in a village outside Edinburgh, in which an eighty-seven-year-old man declared: 'I am not dead and never have been.' Local villagers had been passing on their condolences to his family after hearing that he had passed away. It became clear that somehow a rumour had spread that he had died, and it was the local newsagent's he chose as the place to set the record straight, as he had always thought of it as being the focal point of the community. Everyone he knew went to the shop a couple of times a week, so it was the easiest way of confirming the not unreasonable piece of information that he was not dead and never had been.

Another story featured a photograph of a newsagent's window and the heading 'Find a Woman for this Man'. A seventy-year-old man had written out an advert and put it in the window trying to find a lady friend. He set out his specifications: *Must be aged 60–65 (ish). Must be fun-loving, a good listener, a bit nutty and not talk too much.* And this had got people talking, the story spread across the Internet and was published in *The Times.*

In Fareham, Hampshire, there was a newsagent who hated people whistling. A customer tried to buy cigarettes and alleges that the shop owner asked him to leave, as he didn't serve people who whistled. Since that day the shopkeeper was subjected to a 'tuneless conspiracy' with people going to the newsagent every day deliberately whistling as they bought things to provoke him. The newsagent had to close his shop down.

I read about a girl who bought a lottery ticket from the shop she did a paper round for, and one day she had the winning numbers, and despite winning hundreds of thousands of pounds she carried on with her paper round because she felt a sense of loyalty to the newsagent.

Perhaps the most talked about newsagent's window is in Hammersmith. The window is famous throughout Poland as well as in West London. Locally they call it Ściana Płaczu, or 'the Wailing Wall'. The local Polish community use the two windows to look for employment opportunities, often written in Polish. The newsagent's window acts as its own embassy; it is referred to in all Eastern European literature relating to living and working in the UK. A Tory councillor was opposed to the window, claiming it was a public nuisance with the pavements being blocked, the streets littered and passers-by feeling threatened. But his opinion was not shared by the majority, who saw the windows as the heart of a united Europe, a community gathered together – which is what newsagents' windows were always about, a role they have filled for a century.

I started to think it would be interesting to try to create a stir around a newsagent's window in Norwich. Since the first time I responded to an advert, I had been thinking about whether I should post my own. I wanted to place something that would be a talking point, something to take anyone browsing by surprise. I looked around the house trying to find things I could sell: some of Molly's CDs, old jumpers, some of Molly's DVDs, a recent *Viz* magazine, some of Molly's clothes. Nothing seemed right.

I printed out the 'Find a Woman for this Man' article from *The Times* online and placed it on the dining table where I sat to use as my inspiration. I took a stack of blank cards and a felt-tip pen and tried to think of funny ideas, something that would stick out. I sat, pen poised, but my brain wasn't being particularly cooperative. Slightly defeated, I gave up, put my felt tips and blank postcards away and started to watch *Seinfeld* on DVD. No matter how stressed I was or how hard my shift at work had been I knew that watching *Seinfeld* would immediately relax me, everything would be back to normal. And that's when I realized there was something I wanted to do. I smiled to myself at the thought of the idea. I was happiest when I was at home watching *Peep Show* and *Seinfeld* on DVD. I knew what I was going to advertise in newsagents. I wrote out the advert:

Wanted, a co-writer for a sitcom.

I put my shoes on, unlocked my bike from the shed and cycled round to a newsagent. I chose a shop I had never been in before because I would feel I couldn't go in there again. I am easily embarrassed and I wouldn't be able to show my face for fear of being recognized as the guy who put such a pathetic card in the window. It felt right that it was sitcoms I had chosen; it's one of the few things I know about. Sometimes when I watched sitcoms during the day while most people were at work I felt guilty, and thought that I should be doing something more productive: reading a Booker winner or volunteering at a charity shop. But then the whole of the first series of *Fawlty Towers* is shorter than the first *Lord of the Rings* film. You could watch every episode of *Porridge* in less time than it takes to watch the *Star Wars* trilogy, so maybe I wasn't wasting my time as much as I thought I was, maybe it wasn't such a bad thing to spend my afternoons watching Kramer pouring cement into a washing machine and Jerry Seinfeld saying 'What's the deal with airline food?' I thought of all the hours I worked at the hotel, all the bad things that happen every day, and realized we deserve our simple pleasures, even if it is just watching an episode of *Seinfeld*.

I looked at the advert I had made and hoped it would get people talking. It would certainly make a refreshing change from 'man with a van' or 'au pair available for babysitting'. I knew placing the advert was slightly ridiculous, but I was intrigued to see what could happen – my big fear in life is being thought of as one of those people who never tried. I told myself this was a good idea, and that the main reason for placing the sign was out of curiosity, that I was interested to know what kind of person, if anyone, would reply. But deep down, I knew I wanted to find someone I might be able to write with, to sit at a desk with and write down ideas.

This was the first time I had actually placed an advert of my own. As I chained my bike up to the lamp post I felt incredibly awkward at the prospect of handing it over to the newsagent who looked a bit like Danny DeVito. I thought about backing out, retreating home, but knew I had to do it, it was too late to turn around. Nervous excitement is what makes life worth living. It's the reason I chose to live in Vienna; it's the reason I had gone for that massage with Lucy – it is important to do things in life that scare you.

'Can I put this in the window for four weeks please?'

I handed it over face down. Danny DeVito scribbled a date in the corner.

'Two pound.'

I gave him the money, but he turned the advert over and started reading it as he opened the till. Terrified that he might start asking questions, I spluttered a goodbye and walked out of the shop, not even making eye contact.

I watched from the pavement outside as the newsagent walked around the counter and Blu-Tacked my notice up in the window. As I walked away from the shop I wondered how long I should wait before I could expect the first email expressing an interest in writing a sitcom with me. I wondered whether the idea would attract some interest or just be ignored, like the adverts for the Beaver's uniform and the two single beds. I thought about someone browsing the mundane items that are often advertised, the man with his roofing business, rooms to let, part-time cleaners. The next day I took Molly to show her what I'd done. It seemed odd to see the advert in the context of a newsagent's window rather than on my dining-room table.

Molly rolled her eyes, folded her arms.

'You think it's stupid, don't you?'

'I don't get what the point is. There's no way you'll get a reply.'

Standing on the pavement, I realized she was right, it did all seem a bit of a waste of time. But it didn't matter if no one replied, it was important to do things, to make things happen. When I was in Vienna I knew that as I was only there for a year I had to make the most of every day. There was a real sense that every moment mattered and that's how I ended up having what was probably the best year of my life. It felt a long time since I had taken a gamble. In Norwich there was no sense of urgency, at times it felt interminable. This was my way of trying to make it all a bit more interesting.

10

SITCOM CAROLINE

'I've got a reply!' I shouted into Molly's bedroom. She walked in and stood at my computer, shamefully eating her words as she read aloud over my shoulder.

Hi John
Love the idea, I often write sketches for South Park characters, just
for fun. Want to meet up?
Caroline

'Pretty exciting,' I said.

'Are you going to meet her?' Molly asked, presumably ashamed at how sceptical she had been the previous day.

'Of course!'

'I can't believe someone replied,' Molly said, shaking her head. 'She's probably mental. Can I come and spy on her?'

'Probably best not to,' I said, although I did like the idea of Molly hiding behind a broadsheet newspaper on the next table, taking note of what was going on as I met a stranger in a pub.

I replied to Caroline's email, telling her I would be happy to meet at any time that suited her. This was exactly what I wanted; it had made spending the two pounds at the newsagent's worthwhile. I would drop anything to meet Caroline, I would phone in sick if I had to. Caroline emailed back, suggesting a time and a place to meet. She ended the email with links to YouTube clips of some of her favourite comedy programmes: *South Park*, *Ren and Stimpy*, *Family Guy*. I watched them and they were all right, but I didn't LOL as she assured me I would do. I replied with links to clips I liked, and looked forward to meeting her. This was going to be pretty interesting.

I emailed her to say she would find me at the bar that she had suggested and that I'd be wearing a red T-shirt and be drinking a pint of Guinness. I told her I had scruffy brown hair, was six foot tall and in my early twenties.

'I'm old and tubby,' she texted back, 'just as well it's not a blind date!!'

I recognized Caroline immediately, her description had been spot on. She wore big 1980s Deirdre Barlow glasses, and with the bulk of her figure the half pint of orange juice she held in her hand looked like she was drinking from a thimble. I ordered myself a Guinness and sat down.

'It was an odd thing to read in the newsagent's window,' she said.

'I just thought it was a good way to get people interested,' I said, sipping my beer.

'I was with my friend,' Caroline explained, 'we had just been to the chip shop next door to the newsagent's. She saw the advert and said I should reply. I'm always going on to her about sitcoms, but she isn't really interested. We stared at the ad for the whole time we ate our chips, and she persuaded me I should send you an email.'

I hoped I wouldn't prove to be a disappointment.

'Do you write sitcoms for a living?' she asked. I tried to repress a smile at the thought of a professional scriptwriter using newsagents' windows as a legitimate means to find a writing partner.

'No. It's just something I thought I'd try out,' I told her. 'I thought it might be fun.'

And so far it had been. At no point did Caroline suggest it was out of the ordinary to be having a drink with someone she had met due to such odd circumstances. Maybe what we were doing was not as unusual as it first seemed. It wouldn't be the first unusual way comedy writers had met – Galton and Simpson, perhaps the most successful writing partnership in sitcom history, responsible for shows such as *Hancock's Half Hour* and *Steptoe and Son*, met at a tuberculosis sanatorium. Hale and Pace met at a teacher training college. Cannon and Ball met while working as welders. John Osborne and Sitcom Caroline met via a newsagent's window.

'So how much of the sitcom have you written so far?' she asked.

'Er, not too much just yet,' I admitted, although even that was an exaggeration. 'I wanted to find someone I could write with first.'

'What's it about?' Caroline was asking questions I hadn't even thought about.

'I think that would be something we could sort out between us. Maybe we could think of ideas together, start from scratch,' I told her, but even this seemed to disappoint her. I felt like I'd forgotten to do my homework.

'So should we get started?' I said, taking the initiative, and Caroline opened up a notebook from her bag. I hadn't planned this far ahead, my thoughts hadn't expanded beyond just the initial hello.

Caroline took a pen from her bag and looked up at me, expectantly. She seemed so keen and I really tried to match her enthusiasm. I knew all this would almost certainly lead to nothing. We wouldn't be called into the BBC for a meeting, we wouldn't be shown into an office at Channel 4 to discuss who we should cast as the lead characters, who we would use as director. What fascinated me was the process of getting an idea from inside my head onto a script. This is what had made me go to the effort of advertising in a newsagent's window. But it hadn't just been curiosity. I wanted to do something with my life, to have a project to work on, do something exciting. I wasn't sure whether this was something Sitcom Caroline and I could achieve: to create a script, complete with stage directions and character names and a title. But as the Chinese proverb goes: a journey of a thousand miles begins with meeting a stranger in a Norwich pub.

'So, what kind of sitcom should we write?' she asked. 'Where should we set it?'

'I don't mind what we do,' I told her. 'I think the important thing with sitcoms is to have realistic characters, and that it's believable.'

Caroline nodded in approval.

'It would need to be original, too,' I continued, 'something that hasn't been done before.' Again she nodded, and wrote 'believable and original' down in her notebook. Clearly we were on the same wavelength.

'What do you do for a living?' I asked.

'I work for the Job Centre,' she said.

'So what kind of thing does that involve?' I asked. 'What have you been doing today?'

'Interviewing people who are signing on for Jobseeker's Allowance,' she said. 'What about you?'

'I work in a hotel.'

'Really?' Caroline said, sounding excited. 'That would be the perfect setting for a sitcom!'

I thought about mentioning that *Fawlty Towers* had been there already, but let her continue.

'Hotels are full of interesting characters,' she said. She clearly hadn't been to the one I worked at. 'It could be a hotel that has something extra about it,' she continued. 'We could have . . . cows grazing outside. And one of the characters could be . . . a bit deaf, so that people have to repeat things and shout because she keeps mishearing things. And funny things can result from that. Also . . .' she continued, clearly on a roll, 'we could have somebody in our sitcom who predicts the future. I used to work with someone like that, she used to read our palms, tell us what was about to happen to us. Also, I used to work with a nymphomaniac. She would come into work every morning and tell us all her stories from the night before, it was hilarious. I think it's good to write about people we know . . .'

This was everything I had suspected might result from using a newsagent's window to meet a sitcom partner: nymphomaniacs and hearing aids. Everything Caroline had suggested had been ridiculous, but that was fine, we were just throwing ideas around. They'd probably had similar discussions when writing *Frasier*.

It was only a couple of weeks before I had another email in my inbox with the subject heading 'sitcom'.

Hi John
Saw your advert in a newsagent's window, am really intrigued!
Hope to hear from you!
Beth
x

Molly wasn't home, so I wasn't able to summon her triumphantly to my room this time. Instead I printed Beth's email out and left a copy Blu-Tacked to her bedroom door and set off to meet my newest potential co-writer. In her emails she explained she worked for a wildlife magazine and had recently had a book published locally. I couldn't wait to see what she was like.

Once again I stood waiting at the bar, wearing a red T-shirt, drinking a pint of Guinness. I was spending far too much of my time meeting strangers in bars. I don't even like Guinness that much; it's just that I was stuck for unique points to describe myself that would be recognizable to someone. After a couple of false alarms, with people walking in who had the audacity of not wanting to write a sitcom with me, a woman who was unmistakably Beth walked in. She was in her early forties, jet-black hair, skinny jeans, white vest top.

'Hi,' I said to her.

She shook my hand and her eyes said 'So this is the sitcom guy.'

I bought Beth a gin and tonic and we sat down at a table where she told me about her day.

'I'm going to be honest,' she said once the conversation turned to the advert I had placed. 'I've got no interest in writing a sitcom with you.'

'Oh,' I said, slightly taken aback, but it wasn't a big surprise. The way her eyes sparkled suggested that she had come for the spectacle rather than to write with me.

'I just wanted to meet the kind of person who would post an advert like that,' she continued. I sipped my Guinness in the knowledge I'd been rumbled. I dreaded opening the local paper in the next couple of days and seeing the headline 'Local man is an idiot'.

'Is this the first thing relating to newsagents' windows you've done?' Beth asked. I shook my head, but was reluctant to tell her any more.

'What else have you done?' she asked. Beth was friendly, she seemed interested, and so I decided it wouldn't do any harm to tell her the less sinister aspects of my experiences.

'It started when I moved into an unfurnished house and had to buy things.' I told her about the garage sale, and buying the beds from Dan. She raised her eyebrows, urging me to continue. 'And then I went for a massage,' I admitted, like a shamed politician. 'A psychic massage.'

'A psychic massage?' Beth asked. I nodded, and she laughed bubbles through the straw of her gin and tonic.

'She could tell things about me from touching my back. It was pretty scary! She told me about my life while I sat on her settee in my pants.'

Beth roared with laughter. I thought she was going to slap my face with both hands like Eric Morecambe. Her laughter was so loud a group at a nearby table turned their heads to see what was going on.

'Why are you doing all this?' she asked.

'I don't really know,' I admitted. I smiled as she giggled and could imagine myself in the future saying exactly the same thing to a therapist rather than a wildlife journalist, and instead of laughing being unable to stop sobbing.

'Are you interested in journalism?' she asked, composing herself to speak soberly.

'Not really,' I told her.

'You should think about it, I think what you're doing is really interesting. You should definitely carry on with it all,' she said as she finished the drink I had bought her. 'If you don't, I will. As someone interested in people, I think it's brilliant. That's why I came to meet you tonight.'

And I was glad she had done, because over the evening things had started to make sense. Beth's encouragement had not been a big surprise, I had already realized that there was something special about the people I was meeting. It had been an unexpectedly fun night, Beth laughed at practically everything I had said, and I thought back to when I was growing up and remembered that I used to make people laugh all the time. At some stage this had stopped happening, and I had just been content to blend into the background, let other people do the entertaining. I knew I'd been too passive for too long. In Vienna I stood out because I was English, and so had something recognizable, something which made me stand out from the crowd. That was my equivalent of drinking Guinness and wearing a red T-shirt. In Norwich I felt that I had nothing that distinguished me in the same way. Meeting Beth was a reminder to myself that I could be good company if I wanted to. I was going to try to be more like the person Massage Lucy had realized I could be if I wanted. And sitting in the pub with Beth I felt life was getting interesting again.

'Do you want another drink?' I asked, and soon the barman was reaching down the bottle of Bombay Sapphire once more.

11

ST GILES CHURCH

My new mission – to go to church – started as a result of seeing a poster in a newsagent's window that said

Come and join us at the St Giles Church fete.
Bric-a-brac, a tombola stall, home-made
scones and hot dogs.

How could anyone say no?

I arrived at the fete and despite the Norwich drizzle there was an enthusiastic collection of stallholders and men eating hot dogs. A noticeboard revealed that the fete was to help raise funds as the running costs of the church were £589 a week. I was going to have to eat a lot of scones.

A man in religious attire shouted 'Come to our fete' through a megaphone. He seemed young for a man of the cloth, and was clearly uncomfortable at having the burden of shouting at strangers. He was no salesman; he looked like he'd prefer to go inside, put his hands together and close his eyes.

He tried to entice passers-by into his church from the rainy street.

'Come to our fete!' he shouted again and again, but he was executing it in such a bad fashion that you could sense people's pace increase as they walked by. You could almost hear them vow never to go near a church again, denouncing religion on the basis of one man's discomfort. Eternal damnation seemed preferable to a church fete when it was spitting.

'You with the red umbrella!' he shouted at a lady who was walking down the street carrying shopping bags. 'Don't walk away!' he yelled. 'Come and join us! We have hot dogs!'

The lady with the red umbrella carried on with her journey. She clearly did not like sausages as much as me.

I made my way past the pastor and his megaphone and into the warmth of the church. An old couple browsed at a book stall, but the decline of religion in the twenty-first century was obviously affecting turnout at church fetes too. There was a lady at the tombola, wearing a cardigan with embroidered horses. She had a couple of kids with her, and their faces portrayed a disappointment unique to tombola stalls. If the church had to raise £589 a week I thought I should at least buy enough tickets to power the light bulb in the vestry for an hour or so.

The lady manning the stall told me I could draw ten tickets for my two pounds. Winning numbers ended in a zero. I reached my hand into the bucket and withdrew each slowly, trying to make it exciting for her. My first nine tickets were all losing ones, so before I drew my final ticket I paused to create maximum tension. Davina McCall would have been proud of me. You could sense the room fill with anticipation. I was so certain I was about to win I imagined that as I unfolded the final ticket someone would look at it, hold my hand aloft and announce 'We've got a winner!' before parading me on a lap of honour. I thought that as I was giving money to the Church, God might look at me favourably and He would want me to win. I unfolded the final ticket, but that didn't end in a zero either. The lady running the stall did not seem surprised I had not won. I've never won at a tombola, I don't know anyone who has. I can't understand how people who organize tombolas sleep at night.

Despite feeling conned out of a prize, magnanimously I still decided I would go to the church service the next day to see what it was like.

In bed on Sunday morning I felt cosier than ever before, warm and foetal, and couldn't be bothered to get up and go for a wee, never mind try to discover Christianity. Grimly though I got out of bed and accepted that I was going to spend the best part of the morning in a church. I felt I should look smart for the occasion, so put on a shirt and my best trousers and made sure my hair wasn't sticking up at the back. I cycled to the church, chained my bike up outside, took a hymn book from the verger (or whoever it is that hands out hymn books) and sat down on a pew. Surprisingly, considering the turnout at the fete was so poor, the church was almost full, a congregation of perhaps sixty people. Those who sat on the pews in front of me were frail; these were people who had lived through wars and rationing, and I imagined would have been going to church since they were children, when girls wore straw bonnets and boys delivered bread on bicycles. There weren't many people present who would have to pay full-price bus fare.

It was cold inside, and most of those around me kept their coats on. It seems paradoxical that church is one of the few places which dictates that men remove their hats, when it is frequently one of the coldest buildings you can find yourself in. Looking at the bald and balding heads around me, I sensed flat caps and bobble hats would have been appreciated.

'Welcome to you all,' said the church warden as the organ music stopped playing. 'Particular welcome to any visitors,' she continued, and it felt like the whole of the church turned to look at me. After brief church notices – forthcoming events and diaries for sale, we opened our hymn books, the organ started to play and we sang from hymn number 252.

It was over ten years since I had last been to a church service. As children, my sister and I would be taken to church by our mum and dad every Sunday, and although they never had to drag us there kicking and screaming, we rarely sat in the car on Sunday mornings with anything more than glum acquiescence. My memories of church are not of boredom or tedium but the sense of resignation. Ours was a small church attended by a lot of young families, so there were a few children around the same age as us, which meant we could escape to Sunday school while the grown-ups listened to sermons of damnation and Deuteronomy.

My main memory of church services is when I was about twelve and I would sit next to my friend Paul, my best friend from school. Occasionally there would be an opportunity for open prayer, where members of the congregation could pray out loud, confide things that were troubling them to the rest of the church, or tell of loved ones in need, and everyone would listen, and say *Amen* at the end. As someone was saying their prayer curiosity would always get the better of me, and I would want to know the identity of the person divulging such personal information. So while sitting with respectful hands together and eyes closed I would try to catch a glimpse of the person talking by opening one eye, and my pupil would dart like a periscope on a submarine looking for dry land. Occasionally my open eye would meet Paul's open eye, as he was doing the same, and it would result in uncontrollable giggling and both of us getting told off by our dads in the car on the way home.

St Giles Church was different from the church where I spent so many of my childhood Sundays. It was much more vocal, there was much more audience participation. Pastor Darren's prayers and liturgies often prompted a unanimous response of 'Thanks be to God' or 'Glory to You O Lord', which seemingly everyone spoke apart from me. I found it difficult to sit at the back and mind my own business, as had been my plan. I felt self-conscious keeping tight-lipped throughout, while others would blast out choruses of 'Hallelujah'. I was never sure of the words, and even if I did know what they were I wasn't sure whether it was right for me to say them and felt uncomfortable at the sensation of them coming out of my mouth.

I thought back to the days when I sat next to Paul, and I'm sure if he had been with me at St Giles we would have been giggling like schoolboys to hide our own embarrassment. But at a certain age in life you realize you don't laugh as much as you used to, the days when you would just spend hours giggling don't last for ever. You become aware that the times in the past where you laughed so much your eyes watered, and the days at school when you had to put your head in your arms on the desk in front of you to disguise the tears of laughter streaming down your face are just distant memories. Sometimes it was so bad that you had to picture the death of your parents to balance delirium with tragedy just so you would stop smiling so much. Those days end when you're about seventeen and you start to learn about the cost of petrol, tax law, and when the realization dawns that one day you will go grey or bald or both.

Pastor Darren, who seemed much more comfortable at a lectern than holding a megaphone, walked up the aisle singing from a hymn book, and stood still next to me as he sang. I felt like he was about to talk to me, pick on me for not singing along. I felt like a member of the audience at a magic show, unable to relax because of the potential of being strapped to a board and rotated while having knives thrown at me by a man wearing a blindfold.

I found it easier to relax as Pastor Darren stopped singing and began his sermon and everyone could sit down again. But soon story time was over, and suddenly my unease was justified as everyone started to bless each other. I didn't like what was happening. People stood up and embraced the person they were next to. The lady I was sharing a pew with smiled at me, said 'God bless you' and reached out her hand for me to shake. I was terrified, a rabbit in the headlights, and did not know where to look or what to do. I have never wanted to be somewhere else so much. The man in front of me turned round, reached out his hand for me to shake and said 'God bless you'. I wanted to crawl under my pew and close my eyes. But soon everyone was at it, the whole congregation were shaking hands, people were crossing the aisle to make sure every single hand had been shaken, every person had been blessed. I hoped I would be left alone, but there were people blessing me, telling me God loved me, shaking my hand, ruffling my hair, giving me high fives like they were the Fresh Prince of Bel Air. At first I found it uncomfortable, but there was such warmth in people's eyes as they blessed me, such kindness in their handshake, and acknowledgement in their smile. All of these are things I crave. For the first time since my alarm had gone off that morning I didn't feel uncomfortable, and the sun shone brightly through the stained-glass window as everyone sat back down on their seats and we started to recite the Lord's Prayer. Buoyed up at feeling part of the church, I was able to join in. Unlike the hymns, which I had never heard before, a combination of school assemblies and Sunday school meant the words of the prayer were etched on my memory as much as the theme tune to *Friends*, or the Dead Parrot sketch.

After the Lord's Prayer was communion; this too was different from the church I used to go to, where the grown-ups downed a shot of Ribena and tore a piece from a bread roll. I didn't really know what was going on. Those in the first few rows stood up and made their way to the front of the church to see Pastor Darren, who let them drink from his goblet and blessed them. My line of vision soon became obscured by the queue of people which built up as though it was last orders on a Friday night. I felt I should join them, but as more and more people made their way towards the pastor I felt so self-conscious that I decided I couldn't do it. I thought this was the right decision, and strangely I realized I had started to feel comfortable in the church, much more so than I had felt when buying the Beaver's uniform or stretching and gurning at the back of the hall at James Lewis's yoga class.

Yet I couldn't help feeling an infiltrator; church was more than mumbling along to hymns and appreciating biblical allegories. I saw the impact that it had on some people; a man who looked a bit like Ian Hislop crouched down on his knees with his head in his hands, rocking gently, touched by a presence I had never felt. I did not want to lessen what these people were doing, it wasn't right for me to drink their wine. I just stayed where I was, rooted to the pew and nobody was any the wiser. I realized how significant church is to so many people, not just under the same roof as me, but in every village, town, city in the UK and across the world.

Once communion was over, Pastor Darren came back to the stand to close the service with prayer. I closed my eyes as he began.

'Thanks to aid workers. They risk their lives for others. Let us pray for those who are in ill health. Margaret Johnson. Andrew Gibbs. Alan James. Mr McManus. Let's spare a moment's thought for those who will pass away today, and for those who will mourn them. Make us more contented with what we have.'

As gentle organ music played we all stayed seated with our eyes closed, alone with our thoughts. I'm sure we were all thinking of people in our lives who needed to be prayed for. Our own versions of Margaret Johnson. Andrew Gibbs. Alan James.

Mr McManus. My thoughts were on something that had happened earlier in the week at the hotel. One morning, one of the guests, an old man, fell down the stairs. I was working on the reception desk by myself and could see there was a commotion at the bottom of the stairs. The man's wife came to reception and, in shock, tried to explain to me what had happened, barely able to make herself comprehensible. I went through to where her husband had fallen, and saw blood on the carpet, a man on the floor. I fetched the hotel manager, who took control of the situation as I phoned for an ambulance. Minutes later there were sirens outside. A couple of hours later the hospital phoned to say he had died and it was me who took the call. It was the man's family I thought of as I bowed my head and heard people's prayers. And the thought of one moment walking down a flight of stairs, the next moment being in an ambulance. The thought of one moment walking down a flight of stairs with your husband, the next seeing him unconscious on the floor.

After a final hymn, the service was over. At the back of the church two ladies served coffee and biscuits. I placed one Bourbon on my saucer and dunked another as I stood reading the church noticeboard. Pastor Darren had to rush off for a baptism, but his congregation stayed to sip Nescafé and chat about the service. On the back wall was a prayer board, where people could write down the names of loved ones who needed praying for. As friends told each other about what they had been up to since the previous Sunday, I stood by myself, looking at the prayers people had posted on the board. Some of the names were familiar: Margaret Johnson. Andrew Gibbs. Alan James. Mr McManus. I wrote down the name of the lady whose husband had fallen down the stairs and felt comforted at the sight of her name among those being prayed for.

'Is that someone you know?' a voice asked. I looked to see a lady was standing next to me, the same lady I had shared a pew with during the service.

I nodded, and told her about the man falling down the stairs, about taking the phone call from the hospital to be told he had died. I hadn't told anybody about it, not even Molly or my mum and dad. It's hard to crowbar death into a conversation, and I didn't realize the events had affected me as much as they clearly had done.

'He's being prayed for,' my pew friend told me. I nodded; I knew he would be. I felt happy at leaving it in the capable hands of the congregation of St Giles Church. 'Will we see you again next week?' she asked, and I wanted to say yes, but knew it was unlikely I'd be going back, even though it would be good to hear the prayers for the lady at the hotel. Religion did not play a part in my life and I was at best a woolly agnostic. I was really glad I had made the effort to go, I'd enjoyed the service, and felt comfortable in the church, especially when we were all shaking hands and blessing each other. I felt a connection, not particularly to God or any other deity, but after so many Sundays of going to church when I was little I felt it was something comforting and familiar from childhood.

'Maybe,' I told her, 'I'm not sure.'

I ate one more Bourbon biscuit, and walked out of the church. As I unlocked my bicycle and rode back home I thought about religion. I felt better after unburdening things to the lady I had shared a pew with. I looked up at the sky, cloudy but bright. I remembered when I was younger, when I sometimes looked at the sky and was convinced God was about to emerge from the clouds. Sunday school had made my imagination run wild, and I would picture what it would be like when the Apocalypse came – ladders would come down from the sky taking all of the good people to heaven, and the ground would suck all the bad people down to hell. I used to wonder which way I would go, and how it would be embarrassing if I was with one of my friends and I went in one direction and they went in the other. I'd probably go to heaven, because I went to church, and they'd probably go to hell because they didn't, and we'd have to wave goodbye awkwardly at each other, like when you're on an escalator going up in a shopping centre and see someone you know on the next escalator, heading down.

I cycled home, a smile emerging. Church had made me feel good about myself. It was comforting to be around so many good, friendly people, and I hope that if there is a heaven it will be like an airport arrivals' gate, with friends who haven't seen each other for years running into each other's arms, embracing, catching up on old times. A place where the lady whose husband had fallen down the stairs at the hotel could be reunited with him, when Margaret Johnson, Andrew Gibbs, Alan James and Mr McManus would all meet up with friends from school, work colleagues, and the people that loved them.

Back home I opened the fridge but there was nothing to eat. It felt wrong just to boil noodles in a pan or zap something in the microwave. It was Sunday lunchtime – I should be having a proper roast. I'm sure that's what all the other members of the congregation would be doing, right now they'd be pouring home-made gravy over Yorkshire puddings, spooning out generous helpings of stuffing and potatoes, and then satisfiedly patting their full tummies.

'Should we do a roast?' I asked Molly. She nodded her head enthusiastically. This was the best idea either of us had had for months. We walked to the supermarket and filled the basket with roastables. We stopped off at a newsagent and bought a Sunday paper. And for once, I felt I was living my life the way it's supposed to be lived. With the *Observer* sports section sprawled out in front of me on the dining table, and the aroma of goose fat and sage and onion emanating from the kitchen, I was as content as I had been in a long time. I knew I wouldn't go back to church any time soon, but it was nice to be reminded that it would always be there if I ever needed it.

12

ART EXHIBITIONS

'You do realize that if you keep on meeting people from newsagents' windows you will end up in a gimp mask?'

Molly had a point. In the last couple of months I had spent more time in the homes of strangers than in those of my friends.

'You'll end up at a police station, identifying mugshots,' she continued. She had been interested in going around strangers' houses furnishing our house, had enjoyed meeting Donna and Mike, and buying the dining table from Chris. She laughed as loud as anyone when I told her about going for a massage with Lucy, but the Beaver's uniform had raised eyebrows. Things were going too far. Molly didn't think I should meet anyone else, but what I hadn't told her was how much I was enjoying meeting these people, experiencing these things I would never have done otherwise. I was enjoying the novelty. My attitude had changed considerably since being back in Norwich, particularly since the morning the man fell down the stairs. It's hard not to change your outlook on life when its futility is presented to you so closely. I thought of my relative youth and health, and watching films or sitcoms didn't seem the best way to spend a rare day off.

Winter had arrived and at home our heating had stopped working. Our landlord came round with a gas man, who told us the whole system needed replacing, which would take a couple of weeks. It was the coldest winter I could remember, and me and Molly had to resort to huddling around an electric heater. Neither of us had much money, Molly had a job looking after elderly people in a care home, and worked on scripts during her spare time. It wasn't often that we were both home at the same time, but when we were we lived on home-made soup, we learned to bake our own bread, and with cinemas and pubs being out of our price range we were suddenly grateful to have Pete's videos, which we watched wearing hats, layers of jumpers and as many pairs of socks as it was physically possible to put on. So getting out of the house and using the warmth of cafes and museums seemed a good plan. I asked Molly if she wanted to come but she had to go to work, so I went by myself. I was happy to share this side of my newsagent's window life with her, the harmless, normal aspects like going to cafes. I never went as far as introducing her to Sitcom Caroline.

I had seen a few art exhibitions advertised in newsagents' windows and so compiled a list of the more interesting ones. I felt that art was something I should find engaging. As a student I had generic posters of the Smiths and Kurt Cobain Blu-Tacked on the walls of my room in student accommodation, and growing up I had pictures on my bedroom wall of bands and footballers and Rachel from *Friends*, but never anything profound, never anything arty. In our house the only picture we had was Molly's framed photograph of Morrissey, on which she'd written in black marker pen

To Molly
best wishes
love, Morrissey
x

Art was in the Norwich air, and this felt a good way to unwind from the pressures of working life. The first exhibition was at the King of Hearts, a Norwich cafe which prides itself on its bohemian clientele. It hosted evening functions including a water vole society and a group called How to Speak More Eloquently. It had published six of its own poetry books, catered for weddings and civil partnerships, and organized recitals of classical music in the upper hall, which was furnished like a palace, with chandeliers and a grand piano. It was the type of place you could play snakes and ladders and not be disturbed.

I chose a table with a good view of all the landscape paintings around the cafe. I looked at a menu, and to my delight found the answer to a question about caffè latte that I had wanted answering for months since an incident at the hotel. Every Sunday one of our function rooms was hired out to a church group, which was led by the omnipotent Father Michael. It was impossible to get a minute's work done without being inter-rupted by Michael. Early one morning he tried to go through to the bar with a couple of others, who he presumably regarded as his disciples. To extend the biblical analogy, the staff were the lepers. The bar was closed, so Father Michael came to the reception desk and asked where the barman was. I told him that he didn't start his shift for another hour and that the bar was closed so I took his order for him.

Father Michael ordered a caffè latte, and his right-hand man ordered a glass of water and a chicken salad. Another acolyte of Father Michael's, after looking at the menu as scornfully as if it was the *Da Vinci Code*, asked if he could get a toasted ciabatta. I took the order through to the kitchen, where the chefs swore like Derek and Clive about having to prepare a chicken salad at nine o'clock in the morning. As they prepared the food I went to serve the drinks. I didn't know how to use the coffee machine, but to my relief found that there was not only a button which said 'on' but another beneath it, which was marked 'caffè latte'. I gave the priest and his friends their drinks and the chefs sorted out their food. As I walked back to my reception desk I felt I had done myself proud.

But suddenly Father Michael was in front of me again. Omnipotent people are like that.

'I asked for a caffè latte,' he told me, his voice revealing controlled anger. I looked up from the paperwork in front of me.

'That's what I gave you,' I answered. He shook his head.

'This is a café au lait,' he told me. I paused while I digested this information.

'I pressed the button that said caffè latte,' I told him. Father Michael shook his head and looked down at his coffee. A couple approached the desk, suitcases in hand, to check out.

'I suppose this will do,' he said, tutted, and walked back to his congregation of two.

When the barman arrived for his shift, I asked him if he knew the difference between café au lait and caffè latte, but he didn't know. I texted Molly, but she didn't know either. My mum and dad didn't know. I texted the cleverest friends in my mobile phone, but none of them knew. I asked a girl at a party, stuck for a mutual topic of conversation. She didn't know either, and went to find someone else to talk to.

But the King of Hearts was able to give me an answer. A caffè latte is one third espresso, two thirds hot milk. A café au lait is coffee and milk in equal measures. I had clearly short-changed the pastor of some milk.

I turned my concentration to the landscapes. As I looked at them I realized how little attention I pay to art. I never notice pictures on walls in cafes or pubs or in people's homes. In the cafe I made myself look at every picture on the wall; I studied them as though I was going to be questioned on them later that day. I pretended I was a collector, an expert, and tried to work out what I would say about each piece on *Newsnight Review*. The problem I had with the landscapes was that they were just sky with the occasional cloud. The watercolours were no more exciting than looking out the window during long car journeys, the view out of the window while you are chained to a desk at work. It was a beautiful day outside, and I was inside looking at pictures of much duller weather. I could appreciate that they were good, but only in the same way that I can appreciate well-stacked tins of beans in a supermarket, but I wouldn't coo over those, wouldn't expect them to receive National Lottery funding or be well reviewed in the *Sunday Times*.

One painting particularly struck me. It was a watercolour

sunset and evoked the type of emotion which few things can, except maybe a floral tribute on the side of a road. Even skinheads must be moved by an unexpectedly beautiful sunset. Even goths. It was so much more powerful than the other paintings of landscapes. I looked at the price. Forty pounds. If I'd had any money I would have bought it. But I was trying not to spend money on things that weren't vital, although recent evidence would disprove this.

The next advert I had seen was for 'Shoes: The Agony and Ecstasy' – an art exhibition inside Norwich Castle. It's odd where you end up if you let newsagents' windows dictate your day. I paid my pound to the girl on the desk and hoped I'd get my money's worth.

The first display was by Jenny Stolzenberg, the daughter of a survivor of Dachau concentration camp. The exhibition focused on shoes found abandoned in the warehouses of Auschwitz. While she was studying for a degree in ceramics she travelled to Auschwitz on a charity bicycle ride, and it was there that she had the idea of putting the display together. As a survivor her father had a philosophy of 'forgive but do not forget', and it was this she chose as the title of her exhibition. Her inspiration was the footwear worn in concentration camps, that it represented every prisoner as an individual. Stolzenberg made ceramics of the shoes that had been left behind at Auschwitz, many of them broken and damaged, and suggested that 'each shoe speaks eloquently of its owner and gives back the dignity taken away from them'. On one of the information boards, Stolzenberg's text showed how evocative shoes can be:

'in many accounts of survivors there was invariably a story about shoes. They caused pain, infection and death, but more happily they saved lives.' It was not just shoes that were found in the Auschwitz warehouses, there had been spectacles, human hair, suitcases.

The next part of the exhibition changed tone, and focused on shoe-based trivia: the average woman's shoe collection is valued at £900; the earliest recognized shoe was a bag of skin gathered round the foot and fastened with animal gut; Marilyn Monroe cut a quarter off one heel which gave her the famous wiggle; in Manhattan it is commonplace to have your feet sculpted to suit your shoes; high heels lead to the shortening of your Achilles tendon.

The exhibition was full of theories suggesting what we wear on our feet says a lot about who we are. I looked down at my own feet, my trainers were battered and falling apart. I decided it was time to leave before anybody noticed.

To finish off the day was Bruce Aitchinson's exhibition at Norwich Theatre Royal which I had seen advertised in the newsagent's window on Unthank Road. I had spent the whole day being arty, but felt invigorated by the one third of espresso to two thirds of milk in the King of Hearts and the platform shoes and stilettos in the castle, so decided to go and see some more artwork. In one afternoon I was trying to make up for a lifetime of shunning the art world.

As it was almost 5 p.m., I expected the gallery to be closed and to be turned away, but I decided to give it a go anyway. The girl at the box office directed me up the stairs and I walked past theatre staff in banqueting uniforms lighting candles in the centre of pristinely white tables decked out with silver service. Not for the first time that day I felt I was too scruffy, holes in my shoes, my shirt untucked.

Bruce Aitchinson likes apples. His favourites are green ones in a bowl. At first his exhibition appeared too much like a GCSE art project; some of his apples did not really look like apples, certainly not the ones that I eat, which are green, shiny and round, and not with the jagged edges he had painted in. Other paintings in his exhibition included watercolour landscapes – pictures of bridges, rivers, the ubiquitous swan. One painting really stood out, though. It was stunning, and would become as synonymous with Aitchinson as Van Gogh with *Sunflowers*, as Edvard Munch with *The Scream*, or Rolf Harris with his *Rolfaroo*. It was a pencil drawing of a girl, sat on the edge of an unmade bed with her back to the artist, wearing nothing but underwear. The picture was telling a story, there was a past, a present and a future within the frame: dejection, isolation, things that remained unsaid. Bowls of apples don't appeal to me, nor swans and stone bridges. No matter how perfectly the artist has caught the light, no matter how discreetly they've captured the likeness, or how neatly they've coloured it in without going over the edges, it will pass me by. For me, life is about people and the stories that they tell. It's like the film *We Were Soldiers*, which was in the collection I bought from Pete. The war scenes with grenades and machines guns blazing made no connection with me. It was the postman delivering telegrams to notify the wives of soldiers that their husbands were not coming home that made me feel something. When he looked at her and said, 'I don't like my job, ma'am.' That postman would have been a much more interesting central character than Mel Gibson as hero.

On display beside the final picture was a handwritten note signed by the artist. He explained that it was his first exhibition for several years and he had not had much time for painting as he worked full time at the Norfolk and Norwich Hospital. Massage Lucy had told me I had unfulfilled ambitions, but I think that is true of most people. Perhaps not for Bruce Aitchinson though, who had a full-time job but was managing to create enough paintings for his own exhibition and arrange with the biggest theatre in Norwich to have them on display. The price list revealed that he had sold six of his seventy paintings and made £230. As I walked back to my cold, cold house, to the next of Pete's videos and another batch of home-made soup, I felt more positive about life, and hoped that Aitchinson would sell all seventy.

13

BUYING A CAR

'It's good as new,' Anthony told me, opening the door on the driver's side. I poked my head in, inspected the mileage and tried to let out a convincing *hmmm*. We were stood on Anthony's driveway and I was pretending I knew about cars.

'L reg,' I said, looking at the numberplate. Anthony nodded, stretching an arm across the roof of the red Ford Escort he was trying to sell.

'Seventy-five thousand miles,' I said. Anthony nodded. I'd never owned a car before or tried to buy one, and had no idea whether 75,000 miles was a good or bad thing, or how relevant it was that it was an L reg. I sensed that this was already obvious to Anthony.

'Can I hear the engine?' I asked, purely out of desperation to appear confident in my role; it seemed as legitimate a request as any before buying a used car. Anthony reached in and turned the ignition. The car went *brum*. I nodded an assured approval.

When I had written down the details of the car and phoned Anthony, I had decided I would just meet up with him out of curiosity, there was no way I could afford to buy a car. I could barely afford to buy food, and certainly couldn't justify cruising around Norwich in a Ford Escort, tooting the horn like Mr Toad. But for some reason when I left my house to walk to Anthony's, I found myself stopping off at the cashpoint to withdraw yet more of my dwindling savings. I pressed the button that said £200 and tried not to think of all the things I should have been spending the money on instead: a haircut, council tax bills, new shoes. For some reason I really wanted this car. I told myself that it would make my life substantially better, that life without it would be intolerable. It had been two days since I had looked at a newsagent's window and seen the details of a Ford Escort written out on a piece of card. It was being sold for £280 and I thought I would take a look out of interest, to see whether I could strike a deal and get a bargain. I wasn't going to buy it though, I knew I couldn't even afford to flag down a cab.

'Works perfectly every time,' Anthony continued, twisting the key in the ignition. It was a sunny day. I wondered whether the car would start so easily at six in the morning in January snow. Already I was doubting what Anthony was telling me. When I had first met him and we were standing on his doorstep he had seemed a likeable enough man, but just five minutes later, as soon as the ignition turned, I realized he was essentially a second-hand car salesman and for all I knew he could be about to sell me a piece of junk.

'I fucking love cars,' Anthony said, in lad's mag parlance, tapping the roof of his Escort with the palm of his hand. 'More than anything else in life.' Despite his cussing he had a friendly enough demeanour, ripped jeans, red and white checked shirt, and looked like he wouldn't think twice about supersizing a Big Mac meal.

'Classic cars,' he continued. 'I'd bought and sold two cars before I even passed my test. Every penny I earned at work I put straight back into cars, and spent all my spare time reconditioning them or just bezzing around. If anyone wanted a lift anywhere they knew they could always get one from me any time of the day. My dad's a mechanic, owned a garage, and I was always going to take over when he retired. It didn't work out like that though,' he said, his voice trailing off, and it clearly wasn't an avenue to pursue.

'So how come you're selling?' I asked.

'It's a long story,' he said, and chuckled, perhaps wondering whether it was one he was going to tell me. 'I got divorced a couple of years ago. My fault. Now my wife . . .' he corrected himself with a grimace, '*ex*-wife, is moving to Chicago. She's been offered a job there, it's where her company's head office is. If I want to see my kids, I have to go too. So that's what I'm doing.'

I didn't know what to say but Anthony didn't expect me to join in. He chuckled at the absurdity, and shook his head. It was clear he was still coming to terms with the dramatic change his life was taking.

'I refuse to be a part-time dad. I'm getting rid of everything I own,' he said. 'I've not really got any choice,' he continued. 'It could be a good thing. I've lived in the same house all my life, it would do me good to make a new start. I've always wanted to go to America. I love the cars, the highways, the "gas" stations.' He chuckled at his Americanism. 'Obviously if I'd stayed I'd be able to speak to my kids on Skype and email them all the time. It's what I do now almost every day. But it's one thing talking to them online when you know you can see them at the weekend, pick them up, give them a cuddle. I couldn't face knowing they were on the other side of the world and that I wouldn't have that regular contact. So I'm selling everything and flying out as soon as I can.'

'Wow,' I said. 'Have you managed to sell a lot of your stuff?'

'I've sold one of my cars. I had two – a Triumph Dolomite, that I sold last week. And this.' He patted the roof of the Escort, beating out a tinny percussion. 'It's solid, reliable, cheap to fill and won't need any attention. It's great if you just want something to drive around Norwich.'

I had been sucked in. I felt Anthony's destiny was in my hands. If I bought his car he would be able to carry on with his life, go to Chicago, be near his kids. I had to buy the car – I wanted things to be easy for him. I was being naive but it felt right. Compared with Anthony's plight this was the tiniest of sacrifices.

'How much are you selling for?' I asked.

'Two eighty.'

I didn't want to pay the full whack. It was time to barter.

'I can't really go higher than two hundred,' I told him, flexing my muscles at being a hard-ass negotiator. I had a lot of sympathy for Anthony, but my financial situation meant I was a few years away from a life of philanthropy.

'I'm not selling it for anything less than two eighty,' he said, in a tone that I feared I wouldn't be able to match. 'I really need the full price,' he said, milking as much melancholy from the situation as he could. Once again, he was Mr Used Car Sales-man. 'I've already reduced it considerably. And it is taxed and MOT'd. It's worth much more than you'll be paying for it.'

'Well I've got two hundred on me now,' I told him. 'I could pay that now.'

He folded his arms. This was a chess match. I was attacking with all the pieces at my disposal, but he was defending stoically and had swiped my queen when I wasn't looking. I took my wallet out of my pocket, barely recognizable as my own with such a bulge of twenty-pound notes. I was hitting him with the visuals. I wanted him to smell my money, to look Queen Elizabeth in the face. Anthony looked at my cash and I could tell he wanted to have it for himself, to throw it in the air like a TV quiz-show winner. He could get halfway to Chicago on two hundred pounds. His arms remained folded though. I am no expert on body language but I think this means *You'll be going to the cashpoint pretty soon.*

'I could drive you to the cashpoint?' he offered. There was no way I was going to get out of this.

'OK,' I said, and put my wallet back in my pocket. Anthony walked back up the steps outside his house to lock up the front door and I stood there knowing I should have persevered with my refusal to go higher. This wasn't going well. Negotiating is not my strong point, the thought of confrontation makes me palpitate with fear. My bank account was starting to worry me, the figures were sparse, this transaction would make a serious financial situation dangerous. I was earning money now, which I hadn't been when I first moved into the unfurnished house with Molly, but even so I was only scraping minimum wage.

Although, having said that, when you added on tips . . . I was still only scraping minimum wage. I was once given just twenty pence for carrying a lady's suitcase to her room. A Norwich industrial estate is a long way from Mayfair and Park Lane. I used to hope that by my mid-twenties I would be living a lavish lifestyle, where I would wear tailor-made suits, have a basement full of red wine and have my own snooker table.

With the house locked up, Anthony got in the car and stretched across to let me in. The car stank, a pungent smell that had once been vanilla, amalgamated with a reek of stale tobacco and armpits. This, through alchemy, formed the smell of disappointment. Anthony and I put on our seat belts; I held my breath and as the engine started Beethoven kept us company on Classic FM.

'Should I turn it off?' Anthony asked.

'It's fine,' I said. I wasn't in the mood for conversation, I needed the time to think about what was happening. It still wasn't too late to back out. I could be honest with him, say I had changed my mind. This was a situation to say a resounding 'no' rather than a feeble 'yes'. That's what any sensible person would have done.

As we drove the realization that very soon this car would belong to me made me feel a bit sick. I started to panic about money; I was going to have to carry a lot of suitcases to earn enough twenty-pence pieces to afford the insurance, not to mention petrol, tax, MOT. At the cashpoint I took out eighty pounds, decided not to check my balance, and put it with the two hundred pounds I already had in my pocket. I was actually going to go through with it. I got back in the car and Anthony drove back, parked outside his house where he took out the relevant documents from the glove compartment. He filled in various sections with the expertise you would expect from someone who has bought and sold so many cars, and handed the papers across for me to sign. I flashed my signature in the spaces Anthony had marked.

'All done,' he said, and I handed over my cash like a blackmail victim. He counted it, recounted it, and put it in his pocket.

'It's all yours,' he told me, and as he got out of the car he beamed a smile, like a poker player trying to conceal a royal flush. I opened my door and got out too.

'Congratulations,' he said, but neither of us were in a celebratory mood. 'A word of advice,' he added, 'the passenger's door only opens from the inside.'

This seemed sneaky, I felt it was a bit sly not to have told me about the car's faults until money had changed hands, but I guess I was getting what I deserved. I convinced myself that this was nothing more than a minor handicap. It wasn't such a disaster. It's good for a car to have its unique characteristics – this was mine. He smiled and handed me the keys. They didn't feel right in my hand. He hadn't even taken off his key ring – Mickey Mouse in a magician's hat. Anthony seemed desperate to get rid of the car and already I knew I had made the wrong choice, that this was too expensive to buy on impulse, it wasn't a new DVD or a big Toblerone or a sneaky post-work pint. It was a car, the sort of thing people save up for all year round, reading every page of *What Car?* magazine, going from dealer to dealer looking for the best bargain, walking away if their demands are not met. People don't phone up a bloke who's put a card in the newsagent's window and say yes to anything he suggests.

'Good luck with everything in Chicago,' I said to Anthony as he walked towards his house.

'Cheers,' he said, turning around, as though I'd simply given him a lift home. 'Let me know if you have any questions,' he said, walking up his garden path.

I told him I would, and walked to the car, patting it on the roof to let it know it had a new owner. I climbed in, put on my seat belt, and as I turned the ignition could see Anthony standing on his doorstep making a call on his mobile phone. I was worried that he was mocking me to one of his friends. I feared black smoke and loud bangs. I could not switch the engine on, not through any mechanical failure, but because I was so aware of the audience. I wasn't sure I could remember how to drive.

It had been a couple of years since I'd been in a driving seat. In fact, despite it being seven years since I had passed my test, I had barely driven enough to have used a full tank of petrol. I'd never driven in Norwich, not driven in a city even. Buying your first car is supposed to be one of the defining moments of your life. This had proved to be something memorable, but for all the wrong reasons. This wasn't something I would be telling my grandchildren about. Anthony went inside and I managed to find the courage to start the car, for no reason other than to get as far from his house as possible. The radio came on as I turned the ignition: Classic FM was playing the *Ride of the Valkyries*. My life was becoming far too cinematic.

I switched off the radio and pulled away from the kerb without stalling or crunching the gearbox and the journey back to my house had started, a journey I didn't want to do for so many reasons.

The smell in the car was worse than I'd first thought. Dangling from the steering wheel was an air freshener Anthony had left behind. I threw the Ambi Pur into the glove box and wound down the windows, trying not to gag. The glove box was in a disgusting state; there were sweet wrappers, tissues, empty bottles, dead things. I vowed it would remain closed as long as the car was mine. It could be a surprise for the next owner, if the car was ever in a condition to sell, and if anyone other than me would be stupid enough to buy it.

Driving didn't seem as strange as I had feared, but after joining the main road I hadn't even found fourth gear when an ambulance appeared in my rear-view mirror, its sirens panicking me like a Second World War veteran. I had to swerve across a line of traffic to the kerb, screaming like a little girl on a roller coaster. Well perhaps I didn't *have* to drive across a line of traffic screaming, but that's how I sometimes choose to cope with stressful situations. After negotiating the crisis of the sirens and feeling relieved I hadn't crashed despite driving for almost a whole mile, I looked at the dials on the panel by the steering wheel and saw I was running out of petrol. The gauge was hovering so close to empty that I panicked and convinced myself there was no chance I would make it all the way home. I was scared my car was going to come to a halt by the roundabout, blocking three lanes of traffic while I was on the phone to a breakdown company, struggling to make my voice audible through the beeping horns, sobbing and road rage. I worked out where the nearest petrol station was, and in the forecourt had to make a brief phone call. I rang Anthony to ask a quick question.

'Unleaded,' he told me. I should probably have asked what fuel the car took before I drove away from his house. This proved, if proof was needed, that I was in no state to own a car. The world already had too many drivers; it had just gained another amateur, getting in the wrong lane, forgetting to indicate at roundabouts, not checking his blind spot before overtaking. But I shrugged off the incidents of the journey, parked by the kerb outside my house and went in to tell Molly about my brand-new car.

'You're an idiot,' she told me.

'I know,' I said, wanting to sink into the ground. I knew the car was just going to stay abandoned on the kerb outside my house. I couldn't even afford another tank of petrol. Already my car was like a tattoo I was desperate to scrub off. It was useless, I knew I wouldn't be driving anywhere, there were going to be no Kerouacian road trips or cross-country journeys to see long-lost friends. I didn't have the time.

'It's because the guy that sold it has to move to Chicago,' I explained. I brought Molly up to speed with the plight of a stranger, and she seemed genuinely sympathetic.

'You're still an idiot though,' Molly told me. But I wasn't sure she was right, I was starting to feel protective towards my car, and maybe there was a chance I wasn't an idiot. Just because I didn't need one right now, just because I couldn't afford one, didn't mean that I shouldn't have one. This was a good thing. It was my growing fascination with newsagents' windows that had led me to go round and look at the car. And it would be useful, I could drive to work, I could visit my mum and dad. I could make journeys I'd never been able to previously.

But maybe I was just trying to justify things to myself. Deep down I knew I was an idiot. How else would you describe someone who managed to buy a car accidentally?

PART TWO

FOR SALE:
Everything I've ever
bought from NEWSAGENTS'
WINDOWS.

14

NEW YEAR'S DAY

I woke early on the morning of the 1st of January and my mouth tasted like something had died in it. Molly and I had invited friends round to celebrate the first New Year in our new house. We drank red wine, ate chorizo, drank rum, sang Pogues' songs, drank Jack Daniel's. I came third in musical chairs and slept in my clothes.

I wiped the sleep from my eyes and the confusion from my head, cleaned my teeth for what seemed like half an hour, had a shower until the water ran cold and then went out for a walk, desperate to get out of the house. I have always dreaded the New Year, January can be so bleak. It's like a nightclub when they turn the lights on; it's a bus replacement service lumbering its way towards spring. Outside, the Norwich air was cold and fresh and I walked on to try to clear my head. For years people have tried to develop the perfect hangover cure, but I've always found a combination of fresh air, self-loathing and a can of Dr Pepper tends to do the trick.

It was a chilly morning and people were out enjoying New Year strolls, leaving vapour trails of frosted breath in the cold air.

With no plans for the day, and no real plans for the year, I decided to plot out a route for the morning, and found myself heading in the direction of Anthony's house. Gratifyingly, there was a For Sale sign outside his house, which satisfied a mild curiosity I'd had over the last few weeks. It wasn't that I thought he was lying, that he had made up the story to improve his chances of selling the car, but I'd told the story a couple of times, and that tended to be people's verdict – that I was too soft, that people like me are a conman's dream. The For Sale sign was proof that what he'd told me was the truth, that he was intent on a new start in America, and I hadn't fallen for a trick. I wondered whether I should buy the house too.

I was in the mood to do healthy things, and from Anthony's I walked and walked, across the city centre, through the cathedral grounds and down by the river. It was really beautiful, I wished I could do watercolours like Bruce Aitchinson, sit down with an easel and spend the afternoon painting. Instead I carried on walking, and found myself in a part of Norwich I had never been to. It wasn't long before I had found a new newsagent, with a window full of new opportunities. And this one did not disappoint, I saw an advert selling 'unwanted Christmas presents'. It was only a week since Christmas, the binmen wouldn't have had a chance to go on their rounds to empty the wheelie bins of discarded wrapping paper and already people were selling the gifts they had no use for. Another advert, in what looked like a child's handwriting, poignantly sought 'lost Christmas mittens, only worn once'. Then I noticed an ad in the window that offered me something more productive to do for the rest of the day:

New Year's Day
Norwich Pops Orchestra presents a Viennese orchestral spectacular,
3 p.m., St Andrew's Hall.

I scribbled the details down in the diary my grandma had given me for Christmas. I didn't have any background in classical music or orchestras, but thought it could be worth checking out. If there was one rule I had imposed on myself over the last few months it was that the more resistant I felt towards doing something, the more reason there was to do it. I wasn't sure whether I would enjoy it, but I would only have spent the rest of the day feeling sorry for myself anyway. And it meant I could delay going back to my house and the mess of New Year's Eve. There would inevitably be wine stains on the carpet and walls, bottles to clear away, and crumbs that would need sucking up by our vacuum cleaner, one of the bargains we had bought from Mike and Donna's garage sale. I decided I would let Molly deal with the aftermath of cleaning, scrubbing and bleaching – I was on my way to watch the Norwich Pops Orchestra.

It was only midday so I walked to a pub that was showing football. My brain did not feel equipped to cope with anything more than gazing vacantly at the big screen. A jukebox played Nat King Cole and as the barman brought over my coffee I allowed myself to be swallowed into the cushions of the settee. Then I dunked biscotti. As well as Christmas and New Year the last two weeks of December also included my birthday and that of my sister and three of my friends, which always necessitates excessive socializing. By January I crave nothing more than comfortable settees, trumpets and Nat King Cole. But as tempting as it was to spend the rest of the afternoon falling asleep in a warm pub with a roaring fire, I decided to go to the concert.

The 1st of January is a musical highlight across Europe. On this day in Vienna there is an annual concert with waltzes, polkas and marches, and it has gradually been replicated in cities across the world, which now reached as far as East Anglia. Millions enjoy the traditional sounds of the Strauss family as well as other Austrian composers who even I have heard of, such as Schubert and Mozart, and now I was going to have my chance to soak up the Viennese culture.

St Andrew's Hall is a spectacular fourteenth-century Grade I building with a high beamed roof, arched columns and a capacity for up to 1,200 people. Its interior would not be out of place even amongst the architecture of Vienna. It seems that St Andrew, the first Apostle and brother of St Peter, must have hung around Norwich quite a lot; not only is St Andrew's Hall named after him, but there is a pub, a church and a car park all bearing his brand name. Not even Delia Smith or Alan Partridge have a Norwich car park named after them.

I left the pub and made my way towards the hall, intrigued by what was going to happen during the rest of the afternoon. This seemed an appropriate way to be spending New Year's Day, a day I had always tended to waste in the past. As people across the United Kingdom were enrolling at gyms, visiting family members or buying discounted furniture, I was doing something I should have done months ago. When I lived in Vienna I always felt I should experience something traditionally Austrian. I felt an occasional pang of middle-class guilt that I never went to see a concert when I was over there. But I never gave it a chance, I always ended up in the same bar, watching Champions League football. Occasionally on the underground I would see posters advertising the Johann Strauss Orchestra or *The Magic Flute* but I never made the effort to go. In fact, there was a lot of Austrian culture which I did not experience; I never went to an opera, never went skiing or snowboarding, I didn't go to an ice hockey game, never climbed a mountain, never owned a small yappy dog. To make up for it I spent a lot of time sitting in coffee houses eating schnitzel. But I was taking risks now, experiencing new things, starting the new year in a new way.

I watched people flock into St Andrew's Hall and still felt hungover. Clearly it was not only me who had been intrigued by the concert. It was more expensive to get in than I had expected, £16, but by the look of the audience around me, money was not an issue for them. These were the kind of people who would spend £16 on a decent glass of cognac. The higher echelons of society were in attendance for the New Year spectacular: brigadiers, war heroes, handsome couples arm in arm. All were dressed in Sunday best, and I felt slightly ashamed in jeans and a tatty brown duffel coat with a bright-red face, and probably looking as if I'd spent the night crying in a hedge. The ladies were dressed like Hollywood starlets, with not a hair out of place, and the best skirts money could buy in the finest department stores of East Anglia; they linked arms with their husbands, who wore shirts ironed specially for the occasion, with ties or cravats, depending on their age, class or eccentricity. I thought of them Brylcreeming their hair in the mirror, polishing their best shoes, putting on their cuff links. I was pretty certain that each of these couples had rowed on their way to St Andrew's Hall, but now they had arrived and were on their best behaviour, about to enjoy the Viennese Orchestral Spectacular.

Some of the couples had brought their children along. I felt a bit sorry for them; they would have been happier if they had been allowed to stay at home and play with their Christmas toys. They were dressed as smartly as their mums and dads, which seemed wrong. I don't think it's right to see children dressed as adults. Even at classical music concerts they should be allowed to dress like kids, a little boy in a suit impresses no one. I imagined how resentful I would have been when I was little, not only to be told I was going to have to spend the whole afternoon listening to the works of dead Austrian composers, but also that I had to change out of my T-shirt and tracksuit bottoms and wriggle into a suit.

I made my way into the hall and paid my entrance fee with the last of the Christmas money in my wallet. They did not accept HMV vouchers. I sat next to a man wearing a tuxedo, who had his hand on the knee of a girl. Both of them looked about my age. It was weird to see people living such different lives from mine. He had a classical music face and his hair was gelled down in a classical music side parting and he was wearing a bow tie. A single button on his jacket probably cost more than any suit I had ever owned. I bet he'd never even seen *The Mighty Boosh*. I looked at the girl sat beside him and failed to see what she saw in him and wondered why she didn't run away with me. My hangover was defeating me. I was passively taking my anger out on others. I wanted to go home.

*

At New Year it is customary to look back at the previous twelve months and think about what you would like for the year ahead. I thought about what I had been doing the previous New Year's Eve, going round bars in Vienna with Marie. We brought the New Year in watching fireworks over the Danube. But somehow, despite the grandeur and the novelty of being abroad, I preferred it in Norwich. When Molly and I first moved in together the reason I was so intent on pursuing newsagents' windows was because I thought I needed to make new friends, fill every second with something productive. But that wasn't really the case. I loved the time I spent in Vienna; in fact I hadn't fully realized how much until I talked in detail with Leni. But I felt Norwich was the right place to be for the year ahead. I had the occasional brief bout of existential doubts, but deep down I knew I was making progress, things were looking up. It had only been six months since I had been living with my mum and dad, and shortly after that I was plucking up the courage to phone a lady about her son's Beaver uniform. It had certainly been an odd year, but a good one. I was happy at home with Molly and, although there was nothing much tying me down to the area, I had no intention of leaving any time soon. At times I had been uncertain that having your life dictated by newsagents' windows was a good thing, and although financially it had been the worst thing I had ever done, I was still glad I'd done it, even though I had occasional restless nights, when I had nightmares of being chased by pound signs. Even though it had been fun, I had to admit buying the car from Anthony had been pretty stupid.

Soon the concert was finished, and I had managed to stay

awake throughout. Making my way outside, I wondered whether perhaps I should have stayed asleep on the settee in the pub with Nat King Cole. I looked around at all the couples who filed through the back doors, and I felt I was the only person who had come alone. I saw the girl who had accompanied the bow-tied man standing alone outside, smoking a cigarette. She was beautiful, like Scarlett Johansson's more attractive younger sister, and, buoyed up after two hours I'll never get back, I thought of introducing myself, asking her whether she had enjoyed the concert, but I decided not to. She clearly had eyes set on men a few leagues higher than me and I remembered that I stank of rum.

As I walked back home I decided to make some New Year's resolutions. I decided to get fit. No marks for originality as a resolution, but over the last few months I had started to get a bit tubby. Even my mum said so. If I was getting back in contact with Massage Lucy, then I wanted to be able to show her a newer, healthier version of the person in the turquoise Debenhams boxer shorts she had seen a few months earlier. I arrived back home, walked up the stairs. Any evidence of the previous night's party had been removed, empty cans and bottles of booze had been left out for the recycling man, the windows were open as wide as possible in an attempt to bring fresh air inside. I walked into the bathroom, and did something I had promised myself I would do ever since we came back from the garage sale with a set of bathroom scales. I took off my shoes and socks and, like a man going deep-sea diving, held my breath and took the plunge. I looked down as the needle hovered, deciding my fate like a ball rushing round a roulette wheel. The outcome did nothing for my self-esteem, and I jumped off straight away in horror, and wrote down the figure in the notes page at the back of my diary and vowed that by next year it would be lower. It didn't matter how much weight I lost, it was just important that I didn't put any more weight on. If I wanted a girlfriend like the girl at the concert or like Leni I would have to take better care of myself.

My second New Year's resolution was to sort out my finances. I had not opened a bank statement since I had returned to Norwich five months earlier. I kept unopened post in the same drawer as photographs of ex-girlfriends, job rejection letters and rejection letters from ex-girlfriends. It's also the drawer we kept light bulbs in. It was time to get rid of my debts. And so I picked up the envelope of the most recent statement, delivered at the beginning of December like an unwelcome Christmas card. I hacked into it like a chainsaw decapitating dandelion heads. The situation was worse than I had feared. I stared at the debits column like a widow rereading the suicide note. I couldn't work out what had happened. Well, maybe I could – I'd bought a car and a bike and a man's entire video collection, I was paying rent and had furnished my empty house while never earning more than minimum wage – that's what had happened. Thank God that girl outside yoga had given me my fiver back when I dropped it. Every little helps.

I hadn't been able to enjoy Christmas because I had been worrying about money so much. I had missed out on the summer, there had been no holidays abroad or barbecues on the beach for me. While my friends had babies and upgraded their Mercedes and got promoted in their jobs, I had been watching videos, and plotting which advert to reply to next.

And so I made a decision. I would sell my car. But until it was sold I would use newsagents' windows as much as I saw fit. Any event I saw advertised that looked fun I would go to, without any guilt. Life throws up unexpected complications all the time – the man falling down the stairs at the hotel, Anthony having to move to Chicago. I decided to make the most of being relatively young and free. If I saw a card with something I wanted, I would buy it, see who else I could meet, proudly bring the new item back home. I wasn't ready to settle down just yet. Not only did I think I could meet more interesting people, but I was sure I would be able to make some money out of newsagents' windows. I took some pieces of card and wrote out adverts for things I could sell:

Men's bicycle for sale, good as new, two
previous owners, both called John.
Bargain at £40.

I didn't stop there, I sat at the dining table and wrote out more adverts. I took a second piece of card and listed things I owned that I thought I could sell: cuff links for a fiver, a nest of tables for £3, a CD player for £6. What a decadent life I had led; it seemed impossibly cavalier that I had ever needed to own any of these things. It was a surprisingly cathartic experience to feel I was doing something about my debts. I took another piece of card, and this felt like a significant new step in my life – there was one thing that I was desperate to be rid of. My car.

This meant my final New Year's resolution was the most simple: to sell my car. And as soon as it was sold, I would stop using newsagents' windows, carry on with my normal life. But most importantly, up until then I would have fun, take risks, see what might happen. I wrote out the advert, asking £280 for the car, the same price I had paid for it. This was no time to calculate depreciation.

For sale, red Ford Escort, good as new, £280.

15

THE PEOPLE VERSUS TESCO

'Say No to Unthank Tesco' I read on a sign in the newsagent's window – 'Public Inquiry 11th January'. Back at home I looked at the website set up by the Say No-ers. Five thousand people had rallied against plans to open a new store on a plot of ground left derelict after the petrol station that previously occupied it burned down in 2003. Tesco had submitted three separate applications to build a store on the land, but had been rejected on every occasion. It seemed the UK's wealthiest company didn't like to take no for an answer, and persisted with its plans. It was decided the matter would be settled by an independently appointed inspector at a public inquiry.

Intrigued, I decided I would go along to see what was happening. I was sure the locals would turn out in their masses; the Green Party have a strong presence in Norwich, and it was widely felt that a new Tesco would not be a good thing, especially in this part of town. Locally they call this area the 'Golden Triangle' – it's where I lived when I was at university. People are very proud of living there, it is a refreshing contrast to modern identikit housing estates; it's rough round the edges and all the better for it, every house having its own unique look. The residents are made up largely of cardigan wearers – students and pensioners – all living in row after row of terraced housing. Every street seems far too narrow, most aren't wide enough to accommodate parked cars as well as a single lane of traffic. A Norwich driver travels as far in reverse as forwards down these side streets, beckoning at the car they are headlight to headlight with to continue, then moving onto a grass verge to allow it to pass.

The Golden Triangle is defined for me by the lack of net curtains, which makes life easy for the voyeurs of Norwich. People seem quite happy for anyone walking past their homes to peer in and get a snapshot of their life. You can walk down any street and see an old man watching the *Weakest Link*, schoolchildren having piano lessons, mums cooking oven chips. When I picture Norwich, it is not the cathedral or castle I think of, not the boats on the River Wensum, the huge outdoor market or the football team that aren't very good any more. Instead I picture terraced houses with a box of recyclables on the doorstep, a 'Vote Green Party' sign in the garden and my nose pressed up against the window, frosting the glass with my breath.

The inquiry was held at Blackfriar's Hall, a wing attached to St Andrew's Hall where I had been on New Year's Day. Despite being a car owner, I still chose to cycle to the meeting. I was more comfortable on the saddle than in the driver's seat. You can't go on the pavement to avoid traffic in a car. At least you shouldn't do, anyway. As I walked into the hall I was offered a Say No sticker by one of an enthusiastic group of Say No-ers huddled outside the main room, clearly relishing the fight against capitalism. A man wearing a bumbag offered it to me but I turned it down. I thought I'd try to maintain a healthy sense of neutrality throughout, but knew I was unlikely to come out in favour of the store being built. I was sceptical about how useful a new Tesco would be. The more I thought about it the angrier I got. I worried that throughout the UK, shops either side of Tesco stores would be forced to close, have their walls knocked down, as Tesco continually expanded. I worried about the number of premises displaying closed signs. It felt like one day a wrecking ball would arrive and knock down every shop that wasn't a Tesco, and the buildings would disintegrate into the ground, like a community shrugging its shoulders. I turned round and went back to the man to ask for a Say No sticker. I was turning into a political activist. I was like the Norwich Che Guevara.

This was the third and final day of the inquiry and the hall was packed; perhaps a hundred members of the public had turned up to see events come to a conclusion, as well as television cameras from the local news. This was a big event. I sat by myself, but elsewhere in the audience acquaintances shook hands, friends embraced, people who knew each other from Neighbourhood Watch schemes, quangos and book clubs reacquainted them-selves. They all seemed very friendly, made small talk while the men in suits at the front of the room shuffled their papers and prepared for proceedings to begin. I was the youngest in the audience by a generation or two, and I wasn't sure whether this was because a lot of people my age would be at work at ten o'clock on a Thursday morning, or if perhaps younger people don't tend to be opposed to big companies such as Tesco. Those older people who sat around me would have been able to remember sweet shops with weighing scales and glass jars of Midget Gems behind the counter. My generation had grown up to the beep of barcodes, the taste of frozen pizza, and putting pound coins in shopping trolleys.

It began with a warm welcome by Robert Neil Parry, a grey-haired man in a grey suit, who explained he was the inspector for the duration of the case, appointed by the Secretary of State, and that the final decision would be his.

Parry took his seat centre stage and to his left was the Tesco corner, four men in suits and a mountain of paperwork. On the table to Parry's right sat representatives from Norwich City Council, speaking on behalf of those who were opposed to the plans to build the new store. Each side was represented by a lawyer – Steve Morgan for Tesco, and his opponent, William Hicks QC. I had seen Morgan in animated conversation on his mobile phone outside as I walked in. Had I known he was representing Tesco I might have roughed him up a bit, or at least slapped a Say No sticker on his back like a 'kick me' sticker in the school playground.

Today's focus was the People versus Tesco. Taking the stand were councillors, representatives from Friends of the Earth and Norwich Cycling Campaign as well as local residents who all spoke passionately and sincerely. One local mother told the inquiry that if HGVs were going to be delivering milk and fruit and veg at eight o'clock every morning then it would be incredibly dangerous for children walking to school.

Next, a local resident, a member of the proactive Unthank Says No campaign, took to the stand.

'I have lived in the same house since 1977,' he said. He had a big grey beard, woolly blue jumper and I liked to think he had just walked in from his allotment. He spoke sincerely, without notes, and his voice revealed no nerves. 'I do not own a car and I use the Unthank shops every day. The plot of land that Tesco wishes to build on is a derelict eyesore, but that does not mean it should be replaced by a twenty-first-century eyesore. Tesco claim they will increase choice for local residents, but in fact it will reduce choice. Take, for example, Sears newsagent on Unthank Road.'

My ears pricked up. This was *my* newsagent. This was where I had been so often, the newsagent where I had seen the massage advertised, responded to Pete's video collection and seen the card advertising St Giles Church fete.

'Twelve hundred houses have newspapers delivered courtesy of this newsagent,' he continued, 'which has provided a personal service for the community for thirty-five years. They stock magazines of local interest. They hold back newspapers for their customers if they go on holiday. They import newspapers from Ireland, Scotland, Germany, as required by local residents. But we all know that Tesco will sell enough newspapers, cigarettes and sweets to close the store down. Thirty-five years of service will amount to nothing. The benefits the local community enjoys at the moment, that twenty years ago were taken for granted, will be snatched away by Tesco, and never replaced. It would be such a huge relief if Tesco just realized how much we do not want this store!'

His brow gathered beads of sweat as his voice went up and up and he grew more exasperated. He clearly knew he was striking a blow. It was a moving speech. This was the moment the spectators at the inquiry had been waiting for for the last three days. After watching the way the QCs on each side had presented their cases, watching this local resident was refreshing in its simplicity. His delivery was clear, straightforward, heartfelt. He spoke using no legal jargon, no cross-referencing and no hyperbole. It was simply a man saying what he felt, telling us of his fears, speaking up for what he believed in.

The loyal Say No-ers enthusiastically applauded and cheered as he left the stand and returned to his seat. The anti-Tesco campaigners had found their Winston Churchill, their Tony Benn, their Barack Obama. There was no way a new Tesco could be built now; this was it, there was only one member of the public due to speak before the end of the case, and the sound of nails being hammered into Tesco's coffin were almost audible.

The final speaker was a lady of perhaps sixty, who took to the stand, and thanked the inspector for allowing her to do so.

'I can't believe some of the things I have heard today,' she said. 'Unthank Road *badly* needs a Tesco.' Her accent had a faint hint of the United States. The audience took a sharp intake of breath at what they were hearing. An away supporter had infiltrated the home fans, she was wearing a Manchester United shirt in a sea of Norwich City yellow. 'We badly need this. Tesco is always very well stocked, it sells fresh fruit and vegetables, is competitively priced and has good opening hours. I fail to understand why there is such resistance among local residents. Why are people so ideologically opposed to Tesco? Tesco is British and has a track record of success. I imagine all the anti-Tesco people who have been at this inquiry over the last three days will shop at the store if it opens.'

There were murmurs of dissent and a resolute shaking of heads, but I wondered how easy it would be for people to resist shopping at the new Tesco. As soon as milk was five pence a pint cheaper than anywhere else, and chicken Kievs or Pepsi were on special offer, surely people would shop there, regardless of how it affected the local community. When it was Sunday evening and people realized they had run out of bread to make tomorrow's sandwiches they would be grateful for a convenience store that was still open, when previously they would have gone without. Maybe a new Tesco wouldn't be such a bad thing after all. The lady at the stand allowed the Say No-ers to tut and mutter before she carried on.

'This is the twenty-first century and if these other shops cannot survive then that's because they do not deserve to. It's as simple as that. We cannot keep shopping at them for sentimental reasons, they are businesses, not charities. The shops may close down even without a new Tesco opening. The bookshop closed recently, and why did it close? Because it was awful! Why would I ever shop there when I can walk into town and shop in Waterstone's, which is infinitely better stocked, with books at a far more reasonable price. Unthank Road is a commercial area, and it needs to be as competitive as possible. When I first moved here from the United States I used to take photographs to send home to show my family the new life I was living. But I never took photographs of Unthank Road, I wouldn't have wasted the film. This is not a quiet area. We are less than a mile from the city centre and we are on a busy road. We cannot attribute rural village values to city life. If you want to live the way people do in the peaceful countryside, then don't live on Unthank Road!'

Mr Parry, the inspector, asked William Hicks if he would like to cross-examine the witness, but he shook his head, and she walked to her seat to the solitary applause of one man. They smiled at each other, knowing a seed of doubt had been placed in the minds of every person in the room. The tension was tangible. Perhaps, despite all the campaigning, despite my gut instinct, Norwich was going to have another Tesco after all.

Both QCs summed up at length, recapping their main points and drawing on specific incidents of the inquiry, and the inspector brought the event to a close. It had been an interesting day, and Mr Parry told the audience the verdict would be announced in the next two weeks, and passed around a clipboard so we could write our addresses to be notified by post. I looked at the faces of the members of the Say No campaign and they still seemed optimistic about the outcome. Clearly they were less malleable than me and it would take more than the pessimism of an elderly lady to make them think twice about something they were so passionate about.

As I walked home I weighed up the pros and cons of the case as though I was the inspector. I took a slight detour from my normal route and walked down Unthank Road to look at the proposed site and the proximity to the local shops. As I looked around the area I couldn't comprehend that building a Tesco could be a positive step. I felt so attached to the area, I'd only lived there a couple of years, but there were so many whose entire lives were on these streets, it's where they grew up and then settled down, and I could sense how quickly the shops would close down if Tesco was built. I grew up in a bustling market town of 5,000 people, and shortly after a new Tesco opened the butcher's, off-licence, bakery, newsagent and sweet shop all closed down. These shops will never be replaced.

I couldn't understand why the inspector didn't look around the room, see all the people sacrificing their free time and proudly wearing their Say No stickers and say, 'Fair enough, let's all go home, if you don't want a Tesco we won't build it, sorry to have bothered you.' These were ordinary people Tesco was dealing with, people who listen to *The Archers* and read *Inspector Morse* novels and were worried about the decline of a community they had been part of for so long. I worried they might be disappointed, that their hard work and perseverance over the five years since Tesco first announced the proposed store would all be in vain. I thought about the Sears newsagent bundling papers at five o'clock every morning for the last thirty-five years. The paperboys back when it first opened would be in their fifties now, have children who have done paper rounds themselves. I thought about the cards in the newsagent's window, taking people's twenty-five pences every week to help with kittens that had been lost and found and rooms for rent. I started to get sad about the decline of little shops where a bell rings when the door opens, and the shop-keeper knows your name. It wasn't specifically Tesco that these Say No-ers were campaigning against, it was everything that the supermarket embodies – the closing down of rural Britain, of urban communities. Local shops are closing down on every street, the world is moving forward and it seems there is nothing anyone can do about it. But these Norwich people felt they could do something about Tesco building on this site, and were trying to do their bit because it was for the good of the community, the spirit of Unthank Road.

I arrived back home, desperate that when the decision was announced it would be in favour of the locals – the cyclists and shopkeepers – which would mean things could remain the same. I opened the front door and walked up the stairs. Molly was in the kitchen. I put down my bag and started to tell her about my day.

'I think they're going to build a Tesco on Unthank Road,' I told her.

'That'll be handy,' she said, and put a tray of chicken Kievs in the oven.

16

MEETING LENI AGAIN

It was already five months since we had met on the university steps, so I decided to try to meet Leni a second time. She agreed and the next day I was drinking Earl Grey in the King of Hearts cafe, waiting to talk in German once more. Leni walked in and waved as she saw me at the corner table.

'How are you?' she asked, sitting down. She looked even better than the last time we had met – tanned, her hair cut much shorter, which showed off her Jenny Agutter cheekbones. She looked healthy, happy, and, I think, pleased to see me.

'I'm really well,' I said, and meant it. The new year had given me a fresh sense of optimism, and I was pleased I'd made the effort to meet her again. Since our afternoon in the UEA sunshine I had continued to improve my German, or done my best at least. I read a couple of German short stories, bought German newspapers from the man in the market, listened to the Berlin radio station and I was raring to go. This time there was no awkward small talk between Leni and me. Instead of being nervous and stalling for time, I hit her with German straight away, just like I'd been rehearsing in my head since we made the arrangement to meet again. I wanted anyone listening in to our conversation to assume we were German. Before the waiter had even taken Leni's order, I was telling her about what I'd been up to since we last met, about New Year's Eve and buying a car and the man falling down the stairs at the hotel. I spoke only in German, and when I had to pause and struggle to grasp the right word she was patient, tolerating my strained efforts to pluck vocabulary from the air. My technique was similar to the claw of an arcade machine, craning for a cuddly toy but almost inevitably unable to make a grip and haul it in.

After speaking at length about myself I realized that Leni might not be interested in just hearing about my life, so I attempted to find out more about hers.

'Did you go back to Germany for Christmas?' I asked as we started on our second round of Earl Greys. She nodded her head.

'I had to get out of Norwich.'

'Do you not like it here?'

'It's *so* quiet!' Leni's eyes, mouth, hands were all expressive, like someone being given a parking ticket. 'You can't stay out later than 2 a.m.! It's so hard to get to London! Norwich is just the middle of nowhere!' She shook her head in disbelief.

'I think that's why we all like it here,' I said, looking around at the rest of the cafe, people stirring coffees, reading newspapers, watching the world go by out of the window.

'How much longer are you staying here for?'

'Until Easter,' she said.

'And then back to Berlin?'

She nodded.

'It's not that I don't like it here,' she assured me, lowering her voice, smiling at her own outrage. 'It's just that I didn't realize how much I would miss people. I miss my little brother. I miss my housemates. I miss my boyfriend. I feel I'm missing out on life back home. My friends are getting used to life without me. I can't wait to get back. It feels wrong to still be here.'

Leni was describing the exact feelings I had when I lived in Vienna, and she seemed relieved to be able to get it off her chest. I remember the moment I realized I was ready to move back to England. It's hard being away from your friends. You make new ones but they are transient, it's hard to invest in friendships when you know you're going to be back in a different country in a few months and then probably never see any of them again. There are people who go somewhere on holiday and then meet someone in a bar and move in with them a few days later and before they know it they've been there for years, their previous life a distant memory. But I knew that couldn't be me. Although maybe if things had worked out differently with Marie that's exactly what would have happened. I'd have been happy with that.

'What do you want to do in the future?' Leni asked me. 'This time next year? In five years' time, ten years' time?'

I knew the question was only intended to be a way to answer in German, but I couldn't think of what to say. For once it wasn't my lack of linguistic prowess that was a problem, it was that I never really had a plan of what I wanted to do, a path I wanted to follow. I decided to open my mouth and see what came out. Leni would find out my plans at the same time as I did. I took a deep breath.

'This time next year I want to be in a different job. I want to work abroad again. I want to be settled in a proper relationship. In a few years' time I want to have my own house, have a dog, have children, have a shed in the garden.'

I felt really passionate as I said the words. I didn't realize how badly I wanted these things until I told Leni. Somehow she had turned into Freud and had sat there quietly as I allowed my feelings to pour out.

I often find it difficult to express myself, to open up to people. But that's when I'm speaking English – talking in German to Leni meant I felt able to unburden myself. When you learn a new language you can't help but create a new personality. The limits of your vocabulary mean there are only certain words you can say, which means body language and tone become so much more important. I found myself telling Leni things I would never tell people I was close to. I felt I was releasing things that I had pent up inside me. Especially about the year I spent in Vienna. It had been the happiest year of my life, I had a regular source of income, close friends and it was in Vienna I met Marie. Being with Marie was the happiest I had ever been. For the first time it looked like I was going to have everything I wanted. But then I realized we weren't going to be together for ever.

I didn't want that to be the last time we saw each other though. A couple of months later Marie invited me to visit her in Denmark. I spent three days there, during which the two of us lay on the beach, sat in ice-cream cafes, stayed in and cooked for each other, and had the best time I'd ever had. But on the day I flew back to England she said, 'I don't think this is going to work,' and started to cry and I never saw her again. I was distraught. I felt sick. I knew she was right, long-distance relationships are not a great idea. I would have moved to Denmark for her. I would have dropped everything for her. But I never told her that.

Talking to Leni, I realized I had spent far too long living in the past. I had been trying to cling on to something that had left me long ago. I wasn't in Vienna any more, I was in Norwich. I was fairly happy with the way things were going, and things were looking up. The advice Massage Lucy had given me had stayed with me. I was letting things inside be released rather than bottling it all up.

'Thanks for this,' Leni said to me, switching from German to English, I imagine to her own relief as much as to mine. The two of us had developed a bond forged out of a common language – and I thought that this was probably the only time she had been able to express her feelings about being homesick. It seemed it had been as useful for her as it had been for me. I said goodbye to Leni, and when she walked away from the King of Hearts I looked forward to our next lesson, to reading more German stories, and listening to Berlin radio again. I went back to my house, relieved at getting things off my chest. I'm sure Massage Lucy, my loyal necromancer, would say spirits had guided me towards Leni, and that goblins, imps and pucks had been responsible for the two of us drinking tea, nibbling biscotti, and talking about the way we felt living abroad.

Underneath my bed I kept a box, which brimmed with every photograph I'd ever taken, including many from my year in

Austria. I hadn't looked inside since I'd been back in England. Meeting Leni made me see there was nothing wrong with opening up, and I sat on my bedroom floor looking through them. It made me feel a strange mixture of regret, missed opportunities, happy memories and pride at what I'd done.

I put the box back under my bed and saw the light was on in the living room so went through to see what Molly was up to. Sometimes you forget how many benefits there are to living with one of your friends, and I was in the mood to hang out.

'I'm going to open some wine,' I told Molly. 'Do you want some?'

Molly was working on a script at the dining table.

'OK,' she said, and put her laptop to one side. It was a Saturday evening, and neither of us had to go to work in the morning.

'Do you think you'll meet her again?' Molly asked when I told her about my afternoon with Leni.

'I might do.'

'Is she pretty?'

I paused, not wanting my answer to be too immediate. 'Yeah, she is.'

'Are you in love with her?' Molly laughed. She enjoyed asking this kind of question. I felt myself go a little red.

'No. Well, maybe a little bit. She's got a boyfriend though. A *German* boyfriend.'

Molly looked disappointed on my behalf.

'She mentioned him in the cafe today. She said how much she misses him, that she can't wait to see him again. Never mind.'

I swished the wine in my glass and tried to change the subject. I knew it was wrong to think about Leni and Marie. Perhaps I should never have opened the box, I should have forgotten about Marie a long time ago. Massage Lucy had warned me I was in danger of having a breakdown and for the first time I realized she was right. I was on the verge of a quarter-life crisis, and could picture myself in a few years, getting a nun in a head-lock, or sitting at home having a conversation with a glove puppet, sobbing gently.

'What's this?' Molly asked, looking at a newspaper cutting on our dining table.

I looked but couldn't work out what it was, and didn't have any recollection of cutting something out of a newspaper. Then I turned it over. It was the 'Find a Woman for this Man' article from *The Times*. I told Molly about it, the man trying to find love via a newsagent's window.

'Must not talk too much! That's quite funny,' Molly laughed, and then paused as an idea struck her. 'That's what you should do!' she said. 'You should put the same advert up!'

I didn't know if she was being serious or not. I shook my head. 'That would be stupid.'

'It would be funny.'

'No.'

'I think you should. I'll help you. We can do it now.' Molly went through to the kitchen, I heard the sound of a cork popping out of a second bottle of wine.

'Let's make an ad for you,' Molly said, walking back in, passing me one of the glasses of wine, taking a big gulp from the other. She rested her laptop on her knees and started typing away. 'So tell me what characteristics you are looking for in a girl.'

'Molly . . .'

'Let's just do it. Even if you don't put it in a newsagent's window, we should make an advert anyway, for fun. We'll put it on our pinboard.'

Reluctantly, I agreed. I sometimes say yes to things I want to say no to. We started to make an advert. We drank more wine, Molly looked through photographs of me and scanned in any she thought would be good to use in the poster, and soon evening had turned to early morning and on the dining table lay an A4 sheet containing a photograph of me and the heading

WANTED: A WOMAN FOR THIS MAN

Age 21–30 (ish)
MUST BE FUN, A GOOD LISTENER,
A BIT NUTTY
AND NOT TALK TOO MUCH

'So are you going to put it in a newsagent's window?' Molly asked.

'Of course not,' I told her. 'You didn't even change the wording! I'm not sure I've got the same taste in women as a seventy-year-old man.' I took the piece of paper, scrunched it up and threw it across the room into the bin.

'You do know it's on my hard drive now?' Molly asked. 'And I've just bought new printer cartridges and a ream of paper. I can print them off faster than you can throw them away. How many should I do for you? Ten?'

'None?'

I still wasn't certain whether Molly was being serious or not.

'How about if I change the wording? Will you put it up then? I'll take out the line about being nutty. I'll write nice things.'

'No you won't.'

'I will, I'll show you. We can do it together, tell me what you want me to write. Let's put one up in one newsagent's window. For one week? Just to see what happens.'

'No. It's stupid. What if someone I knew saw it? If someone I work with saw it I'd have to quit my job. I'd have to move out of Norwich. There would be no way of explaining it. People I've never even met before will see the picture. I don't want that, it's weird. I'm not sure I'm comfortable at being branded a nobhead by strangers. I'm stopping using newsagents' windows, anyway. I'm getting bored of them.'

'This could be a last thing to do before you stop.'

'No!'

'But it would be funny! You will definitely meet your future wife if you do this. I promise! It's fate. Imagine being able to tell the story about how you met your wife. If you tell that to people in a restaurant you'll be eating there for free, they'll throw in a bottle of champagne. It's heart-warming.'

'But that's not what would happen. No one would reply to it. I'd look stupid.'

'Go on.'

'No.'

'OK,' Molly said, and flipped the lid of her laptop down. 'It would have been fun though.'

'If you'd suggested it six months ago I'd probably have said yes,' I said. I knew Molly would try to make me change my mind, to convince me it would be fun, but I knew there was no way that an advert with a photograph of my sad, desperate face could appear in a newsagent's window.

THE EDINBURGH FESTIVAL

I walked with Caroline to the bus stop. She had been at my house for just over an hour when we admitted defeat. All of the references she had made had completely washed over me – I had never seen an episode of *Ren and Stimpy* and didn't really like *Family Guy* much. In turn she had never even heard of *Brass Eye* or *The Thick of It*. We just didn't have much in common. In the middle of our Venn diagram of comedy the only overlap was Del Boy falling down at the bar. There was no way we could write a sitcom together. It is possibly worth noting that when Ricky Gervais and Stephen Merchant wrote *The Office* it wasn't as a result of meeting via a newsagent's window.

'Has this been OK?' I asked as her bus pulled in. I was worried that I'd provided her with a less than satisfactory outcome.

'Yeah, it's been really fun,' she told me, to my complete surprise. 'I love talking about comedy, it's just the best thing in the world.'

I was slightly taken aback, I had worried she'd found it all a waste of time. It had been Caroline who had suggested meeting for a 'proper writing session' and as I had the house to myself for the weekend I invited her round to mine. I had even bought a whiteboard and a thick black marker especially. I wanted to look the part. But despite having all the props, we didn't really achieve that much. When Caroline left there was still a lot of whiteboard that hadn't been touched, but clearly the time we'd spent talking about Alan Partridge and *Dad's Army* had been more fun for both of us than I had anticipated.

'Bye,' she said, and gave me a hug. She turned around, got on the bus and showed the driver her return ticket, and took a seat at the back. We had agreed to stay in contact, and I really hoped I'd hear from her again. But I knew it was pretty unlikely. As the bus started its engine I walked away, and it was hard not to be disappointed. When I placed the advert I hadn't expected anything to happen, certainly not to have a virtual stranger talking to me about *The Simpsons*, but it had been a pleasant evening, and I looked forward to saying to Molly, 'You'll never guess who came round . . .'

Instead of going back home I called round at my friend Paddy's. I explained about Sitcom Caroline, the grazing goats and the nymphomaniacs.

'Why did you do that?' he asked.

'Because of newsagents' windows.' I'd told him about Massage Lucy and Pete and the videos.

'Yeah, but why a sitcom?'

I wasn't so sure why.

'I guess I thought it might be fun. And I've sometimes thought about having a go at writing a sitcom.'

'Well, we could do that,' Paddy said. 'You don't need to meet strangers who like watching cartoons. We should try one, it'd be fun.'

I hadn't even thought of asking Paddy if he was interested in writing a sitcom with me. As soon as he said it, it seemed obvious. As my head had been wrapped up in newsagents' windows for such a long time, things that should have seemed clear had become confused with the procession of strangers I had been meeting in bars. Common sense lagged behind, which is also an explanation for why I'd bought a car, a Beaver's uniform and attempted to write a sitcom with a woman who seemed to love cartoon characters more than human beings.

I got to know Paddy through my friend Yanny when they lived in a derelict pub. Once they moved in, the pub became a popular venue whenever there was a party to be had: birthdays, stag nights, bar mitzvahs. At the time, Paddy was doing an MA in creative writing. It only lasted a couple of months, his funding soon fell through and he was forced to find a new career as a barman. This was a common route for many creative writing graduates in Norwich – a city of aspiring writers and as many actual bar staff.

Paddy was one of the most naturally funny people I had ever met. He had read more books than me, told better stories than me and was better at Trivial Pursuit than me. When he wasn't polishing glasses and pouring pints, he performed at comedy gigs. His career had started a year earlier, when he became one half of the performance poetry duo Yanny Mac and Pikey Paddy, a joke that started in the derelict pub and ran as far as compèring the Latitude Festival poetry tent alongside such poetry aristocracy as John Hegley and John Cooper Clarke, gaining a minor cult following in the process.

After Latitude, Paddy did gigs with a new creation – Bobby

Dylan. This new character existed entirely because Paddy did a passable impression of Bob Dylan. Bobby Dylan's repertoire would consist of putting a hat on and playing songs such as 'Parklife' by Blur in the style of Bob Dylan.

Every Wednesday there was a cabaret night in the back room of the pub where Paddy worked. This is where Bobby Dylan made his first public appearance, perched on a stool in front of an audience who had paid a pound each for the privilege of hearing his cover versions of Britpop songs. Paddy would play his badly out of tune acoustic guitar, and comically interpret the songs in a drawl that owed more to Paddy's Shropshire than Dylan's twang. The cabaret audience would always be split between those who had no idea of what was going on, and those who had tears of laughter streaming down their faces. The split was around 90–10 in bewilderment's favour. I was in the 10 per cent minority, whose calls for an encore were met by a stern 'no' by the compère. Apparently fifty minutes was enough.

While Paddy was performing comedy, I had started to perform at poetry gigs. At university I had joined the creative writing society, and it was through this that I met people like Molly, Yanny and Paddy, as well as many other Norwich writers, and we got the chance to perform at poetry nights, including the cabaret night at Paddy's pub. Paddy and I started to perform at more and more gigs, often on the same bill, and we would occasionally talk about doing a show together at the Edinburgh Festival Fringe. We knew it was unlikely to be something we would ever do, but we both liked to make grand plans, we had dormant ambitions lurking somewhere that I hoped would come to fruition. Then one day Paddy called to say he had heard of a venue that was looking for its last couple of slots to be filled at the last minute.

'Should we do it?' he asked. I thought about it for a couple of seconds.

'OK,' I said, instinctively. I sometimes say yes to things I should say no to.

'We could do that show about the mid-Nineties?' Paddy suggested.

When we talked about this hypothetical show we would do at a non-specific time in the future, one of the ideas we'd had was that as things such as *Grease*, ABBA and Queen were increasingly popular, we would do a nostalgia comedy poetry show about the mid-Nineties, an era that was never that good in the first place. We were both big fans of Britpop and that era. We'd often fondly remember episodes of *TFI Friday* or our favourite Blur B-sides. Historically, it wasn't the most eventful of times, not something people would reminisce about in the way they did about the Sixties, or punk. And so, against our better judgement, a couple of months later we had written a comedy and poetry show, had printed 5,000 flyers, ordered badges, booked train tickets, and were taking 'The Mid 90s la la la' to the biggest arts festival in the world.

'It's about Blair, Barrymore and Britpop,' we told the people of Edinburgh as we thrust flyers into the hands of anyone who passed our venue. Almost inevitably, people's responses were of confusion. 'Why?' they would often ask, and we were never able to provide a satisfactory answer. Occasionally, someone would seem interested, but that was so rare I can still vividly remember every one of those occasions. Paddy and I had faith in the idea, though, we knew it was something people might like. It was niche, but we assumed that would be to our advantage, one of many fatal misjudgements we made. We performed the show for twenty-eight consecutive days, to an average of fifteen people a day. And when you consider that for one performance we had eighty people in, that means we did a lot of shows where there were as many people in the audience as there were on stage.

Despite this, I loved everything about being in Edinburgh. I loved the whole experience. I felt incredibly proud to be part of something so big, and to have achieved something relatively few people manage. The 'Mid 90s la la la' was an OK show, but could have been a lot better. Our lack of success was entirely our own fault. We blamed our mediocrity on the fact that our venue wasn't great, and that our audience were rarely Britpop savvy enough. But in truth we failed because we had only spent three days writing the script, never working more than two hours a day. We got no reviews, little praise and no money. It seemed the world wasn't yet ready to be nostalgic about the mid-Nineties.

In fact Paddy and I made so little money that summer that in the afternoons after our show we would sit in the Pleasance Courtyard, the hub of the Fringe, unable to afford a pint. On nearby tables sat comedians, Paul Merton at one table, Richard Herring at another. These were people who were largely responsible for our love of comedy and performing, and it was pretty exciting to be in such proximity to our heroes, although it would have been preferable not to be so hard up. While those around us drank merrily, Paddy and I had to resort to pouring Lidl own-brand cider into empty pint glasses under our table, out of the view of the bar staff, trying to make sure we didn't embarrass ourselves in front of Paul Merton and Richard Herring. We did it every day, after every single show, and it was hard not to have the feeling that things shouldn't really be this way. The result of all our toils, all our expense, all the sleepless nights of worry? We got one review. It wasn't from *The Times* or the *Observer* or *Loose Ends*. It was from a man called Steve who wrote on his blog, 'The Mid 90s la la la. Not bad, I suppose. 4 out of 10.' It was a review that made me realize leaving the country a couple of months later to teach English in Vienna was probably for the best.

So it wasn't like me and Paddy were new to working on a project together. In Edinburgh, due to a complete lack of money and alternatives, we stayed at Paddy's auntie's house, where we shared a double bed – a mid-Nineties Morecambe and Wise. But not once in all that time did I suggest to Paddy that we should write a sitcom. Possibly because it felt like we were already in one.

'Let's do it then,' I said to Paddy.

'All right,' he said.

'Not about the mid-Nineties though,' I suggested.

And so it was decided: the next time we met, we would start work on a sitcom. All we needed was a bottle of cider, and ideas would flow.

18

BEDROOM FARCE

'Do you want to go and see an Alan Ayckbourn play?' I asked Molly.

'When?'

'Ten minutes.'

Molly told me she didn't want to, so I went by myself. I'd looked at the newsagents' windows on my way home from work specifically for something to do that evening. It had been a long day and I didn't feel like staying in all night. And then I saw the advert for *Bedroom Farce* and knew I had to be there.

I don't really go to the theatre. When I was about ten I saw Phillip Schofield in *Joseph and the Amazing Technicolor Dreamcoat*, and I went to see *King Lear* on a sixth-form English literature trip. When Paddy and I were at the Edinburgh Festival, despite being there for a whole month, we only went to see one show, a play called *Motherland*. And the only reason we went to see that was because we met two of the actresses at a party. And that's the extent of my life as a theatregoer – A

Level syllabus or unrequited lust. But now newsagents' windows were guiding me, and when I saw a poster in a window advertising the Alan Ayckbourn play *Bedroom Farce* I had to go.

I was looking forward to going; it felt like the type of thing I should be doing. I like to think I'm cultured; I download Radio 4 podcasts, I don't mind watching films with subtitles, I've been to YO! Sushi. But the theatre is entirely alien to me, I wouldn't recognize Derek Jacobi or Alan Bleasdale if we were trapped in a lift together.

I'd always been aware of the Maddermarket Theatre. It's situated in the city centre and is an attractive black and white beamed building I'd walked past plenty of times. But this was the first time I had been inside, and as I stood in line for my ticket I read a leaflet about the Maddermarket: an old-fashioned community theatre that stages 200 productions a year, ranging from one-man shows to orchestras performing Bach symphonies. One of its reasons for being a much-loved theatre is the quality of sound – it has impressive acoustics due to the shape of its roof, based on the Sistine Chapel. I felt quite bad that I had never been, it seemed a worthwhile organization, a non-profit-making registered charity; all the money it earns goes to the theatre's day-to-day running costs. A large part of the theatre's income comes from money left in wills, which has kept it going for almost a century.

I sat in the bar and watched people arrive, smiling in anticipation of the forthcoming entertainment. The room became packed. Close to a hundred people were drinking gin and tonics and white wine spritzers and halves of locally brewed ale and there didn't seem to be a person there under the age of fifty-seven.

Unlike New Year's Day, when I begrudged spending money on watching the Viennese Orchestral Spectacular, I was quite happy to give the woman at the box office ten pounds for my ticket. I chose to sit in the front row as I've got long legs and wanted to give them some room rather than sitting hunched like a Ryanair passenger. I needed every ounce of concentration to watch the play; there was no Molly or Paddy on hand to whisper key plot moments into my ear.

There was a buzz as I walked through to the main room, a pleasant chatter of people catching up. I found my seat, sat down and stretched my legs out like Inspector Gadget. Soon the row was full and I turned round and saw there was barely a spare seat in the house, impressive for a Thursday evening. Being on row A meant that I was so close to the stage I was practically touching the fourth wall. Had it been a stand-up comedian about to come on there is no way I'd have been able to avoid being part of audience participation, answering his questions about what I did for a living in the name of 'banter'. I felt safe that an Alan Ayckbourn play wouldn't involve picking on people in the front row.

'Lots of people,' I said to the man next to me.

'Yes,' he said.

'Is that how it always is here?' I asked.

'Not really. There was a good review in the *Eastern Daily Press* on the first night of this show though. That's why it's full tonight, perhaps. It is already sold out for Friday and Saturday,' he continued. He was smartly dressed – shirt and jacket but no tie. His accent sounded Dutch.

'This is my first time here,' I explained. The man nodded, and in my head this was his way of welcoming me into the fold. 'Do you come here a lot?' I asked.

'Not so much,' he told me. 'I prefer to go to the cinema. I am a pilot, I fly in to Norwich maybe once a week. And so need something to do in the evenings. Sometimes the cinema, sometimes here. Sometimes just the TV in my hotel room.'

Our conversation was ended by the dimming of the house lights. The first scene consisted of a man waiting for his wife to get ready while he checked his watch, worrying they were going to miss their booking at the restaurant. My heart sank a little at the huge appreciative laughs from an audience of men familiar with waiting for their wives, and women in the audience who were accustomed to being tutted at impatiently while they applied mascara. This was not a play targeted at someone in their mid-twenties. It dawned on me that the play might not be very good.

'He's just like you,' a lady behind me whispered to her husband about the curmudgeonly actor. The play changed quickly between all three sets, a different couple in each; newlyweds, middle-aged and old. In a bedroom on the raised platform was a bedridden husband being nursed by his wife. In fact, the actor portrayed the role with such conviction that it looked like he was genuinely suffering, and the audience, with their collection of aching bones, grimaced with empathy as the actor clutched his back while his wife fluffed his pillows. The third couple were twentysomethings who had just moved into their marital home. Man and wife were delighted with every nuance of being with each other. I was interested by the subtext, that inside every old married couple are memories of being newlyweds, who once tickled each other and chased each other through the house and lay in bed with their whole lives ahead of them.

Many of the jokes whooshed over my head and straight into the lap of the target audience behind me, who were more ready to laugh out loud at the idiosyncrasies of middle Britain. But after feeling less than optimistic for the first ten minutes of the play I started to enjoy it; there were plenty of jokes, and at times the whole row shook with laughter, the shaking of ribcages rattling the fixtures of the pews. The intimate nature of the Maddermarket meant that laughter was infectious, the pilot was roaring, and I was laughing out loud without even realizing. It is a special feeling to be surrounded by laughter, to hear the nuances of every individual giggle or guffaw around you. Behind me a lady snorted and perhaps if I was on the bus or in a cafe it would have annoyed me but in the closeness of the theatre it was endearing, hearing the *gh* of every laugh, and seeing wide smiles in my peripheral vision.

The lights dimmed, the actors walked off stage and the audience applauded. It was the interval, and its arrival was timely; I had been drinking coffee all afternoon at work which meant my bladder was as vulnerable as those of the ageing audience around me.

I made my way out, joining the queue snaking out of the auditorium. I was in search of the Gents but couldn't negotiate the rabble pestering the ice-cream man – men and women crowded around, shouting for vanilla, strawberry, mint choc chip like it was the Stock Exchange. This was clearly as much a part of their night out at the theatre as the play itself; scoops of vanilla as integral as the stage, the curtain, the set. I elbowed my way back to my seat, but all the stalls were now completely empty, other than the pilot next to me, eating an ice cream. I felt I was missing out on something, so I made my way to the foyer.

I came back ten mintues later with a tub, a wooden spoon and a feeling of satisfaction. I could tell the pilot was proud of me. People were making their way back to their seats and we were ready to begin.

Not for the first time since I began allowing newsagents' windows to dictate my days I was surrounded by people appreciating the simplicities in life, beauty emerging from the mundane. The scene to close the first half featured a husband reading out *Tom Brown's Schooldays* to his wife in bed, trays of sardines on toast on their knees. The definition of domesticity.

The couple behind me, all vanillaed up, were talking about the merits of sardines on toast.

'Sardines on toast with vinegar,' one suggested.

'And cherry tomatoes.'

'And black pepper.'

Over the next three quarters of an hour there were resolutions and reunifications and soon the actors held hands and bowed, and I was clapping as loudly as anyone. I walked away from the Maddermarket chirpier than ever, my life affirmed by sardines on toast and *Tom Brown's Schooldays* and the stampede for ice cream.

*

'How was it?' Molly asked when I got back home.

'Really good,' I said. 'I met a pilot and ate ice cream.'

Molly nodded. I could tell she was pleased for me.

19

SITCOM

I sat with Paddy at the bar of the disused pub. The brewery hadn't been kind enough to supply unlimited free beer to the pumps, so we had to be content with a big bottle of cider from the shop around the corner. It was midnight, we had been working on our sitcom for almost an hour and had already given ourselves two breaks to check emails. It was a work rate like this that had meant we had been such a roaring success at Edinburgh.

We were having fun though. When I spent time with Caroline the two of us had felt uncomfortable around each other, and struggled to put anything worthwhile on paper, certainly nothing that would make anyone laugh – although that wouldn't have made it so different from most of the sitcoms on television over the last five years. It was much easier working with Paddy, and what we were doing actually felt achievable, that we could write something and send it off to a production company. It was different from writing our Edinburgh Fringe show, which we largely did separately, and emailed what we had written to each other. Most of the time back then was spent panicking and trying to learn our lines. We spent much longer pacing up and down the streets near our venue memorizing our lines than we ever did writing them. Writing a sitcom was turning out to be much more natural, we could set our own agenda, and do it all in our own time. If there was one night when we didn't achieve anything, then that was fine, we'd just do it the next time. Or the time after that. If we wanted to check our emails and talk about football and go to the shop to get more cider, then that wasn't a problem – we had no schedule, no date when an audience would be coming to see us, and we hadn't invested a lot of our savings and a month of our lives in this, as we had done in Edinburgh. The two of us spent a lot of time hanging out anyway, we might as well try to do something productive. We heard keys in the front door of the pub, and Joel, who lived with Paddy, came in.

'What are you two doing?' he asked.

'Writing a sitcom,' we told him.

'Fair enough,' Joel said and went upstairs. It seems the longer you live in a derelict pub, the less surprised you are at what happens inside it.

We had already discussed where to set our sitcom. We wrote down ideas as they came to us, brainstormed anything we thought might work. Sitcoms are such well-trodden ground it is increasingly difficult to reinvent the genre. Especially if you're a bit pissed.

Eventually we settled on a sitcom based on the weekly cabaret night at the pub where Paddy worked, something we had both performed regularly. Each episode would feature a different performer, and follow his day leading up to the evening's gig. This would give us the opportunity to resurrect Bobby Dylan, and other people we had seen performing at the cabaret night could work as characters.

'This is going to be fucking brilliant,' Paddy declared, and I agreed entirely as I refilled my pint glass with cider.

'What should we call it?' I asked.

'How about "Paddy"?' Paddy suggested.

We thought of other titles, and ended up choosing 'Dead Doggerel', for reasons that made sense at the time. We were racing through the sitcom writing process, we had already picked the production company we wanted to work with – Baby Cow. We decided to offer them first refusal. Baby Cow was set up by Steve Coogan and Henry Normal, and was responsible for producing some of the best-known sitcoms of the last few years, including *Gavin & Stacey* and *The Mighty Boosh*. Pleased with pages full of ideas, characters and plots, we put down our bookies' pens and allowed ourselves another break.

'It'll write itself,' Paddy said, and put it to one side and fetched the cider from the fridge. 'I can't wait to be invited to parties at Steve Coogan's house.'

The next day we met again. Disappointingly, the sitcom hadn't written itself, it had been left completely for us to deal with. Paddy had brought his computer down to the bar, and opened up a new blank Word document and typed

Dead Doggerel
Scene 1.

Molly had taught me the right way to format a screenplay so it could be considered for submission, and I had borrowed one of her books called *The Complete Screenplay*. We were an unstoppable force destined to take over the world.

As soon as Paddy started typing we were on a roll. Ideas flowed like ice-cold cider. Without even pausing for an email break we had filled pages with ideas and jokes in little over an hour.

'Fifteen pages,' I said, checking the computer screen. 'That's pretty good.'

'That's all that Baby Cow asked for.'

'Really?'

'Yeah. I checked their website. The worst thing we can do is to edit too much and spoil it. I think we should email Steve Coogan now. While it's still fresh in our minds and seems like a good idea.'

'OK,' I agreed, acknowledging the common sense. And a few minutes later at the click of a button our sitcom was arriving at a submissions office, destined to cause a flutter of excitement in the heart of whoever was lucky enough to read it first. It would be like discovering the Beatles. Or *Men Behaving Badly*.

Ten minutes later we checked our emails again. It was unlikely that they would have replied so quickly, especially as it was one o'clock in the morning, but we thought it was worth making sure. Creative types keep odd hours. And Steve Coogan's probably got a BlackBerry.

'Nothing,' Paddy said, shaking his head.

'I'll check mine,' I told him, but would have been surprised if they had written to me, particularly as we hadn't even included my email address on the submission. I typed in my Yahoo password.

'One email in inbox,' I said, pointing to the screen, and me and Paddy celebrated at such exciting news. But then stopped still. 'Shit,' I said.

'What is it?'

I couldn't explain to Paddy what I'd just read. It was something bad. He leaned over and read out the subject line.

'"Wanted, a woman for this man."'

I scrolled down so Paddy couldn't see what I had just read.

'What is it?' he asked again, and it made sense to just tell him. I was sick of bottling things up and keeping things to myself.

'One of the things I was going to do with newsagents' windows was to place an advert with a photo of myself with the heading "Wanted: A woman for this man",' I explained. 'I told Molly and she mocked up an advert and printed it out, but I made her promise not to put it up and she said she wouldn't, and we never mentioned it again. But I've just got an email from a girl who has seen the advert.'

'You should reply!'

'But it means she put the advert up. She was never supposed to. I told her not to. People will have seen it! I look stupid.'

Paddy tried to talk me down, to tell me it wasn't as bad as I thought. But I was of the opinion that it was exactly as bad as I thought. It was worse than I could comprehend. Slightly influenced by my bellyful of white cider, I phoned Molly, but her phone was switched off.

'I'm going to head off,' I told Paddy. 'Sorry.'

It was a shame that such a historic moment in the world of sitcom had been marred by such a low moment in my life with newsagents' windows. This was bad. So bad. I couldn't believe she had done it. It was six weeks since Molly and I had spent the evening drinking and talking specifically about *not* finding a woman for this man. At first I had a suspicion that Molly might go ahead with it, but I decided it would be pretty unlikely. Clearly I was wrong. I had no idea how to respond. The breakdown Massage Lucy had predicted had suddenly become more likely than either of us had realized. I was going to have to move house. I would have to move back in with my mum and dad. Or maybe I would move back to Germany, go back to Austria, go anywhere as long as it didn't have a newsagent with a picture of my face in its window. Molly had driven me out of Norwich.

'Bye, Paddy,' I said, wheeling my bicycle out of the door.

'I'll call you if Steve Coogan gets in touch,' he assured me.

I cycled home feeling pretty demoralized, and really hoped Molly was in, and still up. I didn't want to have to go to bed without finding out what had happened.

Molly was brushing her teeth. The bathroom door was open.

'You put my advert up,' I said. She saw me in the mirror and stopped brushing. I hate confrontation but this was necessary. I wanted Molly not only to know that I had found out, but to realize how angry it had made me, how let down I felt.

'Why do you say that?' she asked.

'I got an email, just now. I can't believe you did it! You promised you wouldn't.'

Molly rinsed her mouth with water, put her toothbrush back in the pot. She flashed a smile but could see I was upset.

I went to my room and closed the door behind me. I would have slammed it but my hinge was loose and it wouldn't have had the desired sound effect. I had run out of things to say to her, I just sat on my bed, more worried than angry. I pictured my friends laughing, standing at the newsagent's window, pointing at the picture of me. This was horrible. I was going to have to go round first thing in the morning to ask the newsagent to take it down. It was all so humiliating. But what annoyed me most of all was that I knew deep down it was all my own fault. I had got myself into this mess. Molly knocked at my door.

'Can I come in?' she asked. I didn't answer, but watched as the doorknob turned and she came in and sat beside me on my bed.

'John, I didn't put the advert up,' she said. I looked up.

'I did think about it,' she continued. 'I thought about putting it up just for a week, just to see what happened. Maybe even a day if they let me. I was certain it would lead to something, that you would meet a nice girl. I thought that it would help. But I didn't, I honestly didn't, I knew you didn't want me to.'

'But the email . . .'

'It was one of my friends at work. I told her about the advert with the seventy-year-old man, and showed her the version we made for you. She thought it was the funniest thing she'd ever seen, and said she was going to email you and pretend it was a genuine response, but I thought she was just joking. I'm really, really sorry. She's an idiot. I did make her promise she wouldn't do anything. I should have warned you she might, then you wouldn't have had to go through this.'

'So the sign never went up?'

Molly shook her head. I could tell she was upset at what had happened and I knew she hadn't wanted it to go this far.

'Do you promise you're telling the truth?' I asked. She nodded. I was starting to come to terms with the fact that my life hadn't changed dramatically after all. I knew that I should have been furious with her, but I could register nothing other than relief.

'Honestly?' I asked once more, checking to be certain.

'Honestly!' she snapped, with mock anger. 'Beaver's honour!'

I exhaled so deeply with relief it made me dizzy. I knew this version of events was much more realistic. For the first time since getting the email at Paddy's I was able to relax and breathe normally again. I thought about what had happened. It had always been much more likely to turn out to be someone playing a joke, one of Molly's idiot friends. The reason I was so annoyed was because I had left myself exposed – with Beavers' uniforms and sitcoms I was an easy target. They would have been stupid not to have taken advantage of my situation.

'You're a twat,' I told her.

Molly nodded. We were both twats.

20

SHERINGHAM

Once the air was cleared with Molly, life started to seem much easier. After work the next evening I unchained my bike from outside the hotel, and my phone rang, the number withheld. I was in a rush to get back home, but I had a feeling the call might be an important one. It would probably be Baby Cow desperate to chat in detail about the sitcom, so rather than letting it go through to voicemail I answered.

'Hello?'

'Hello. Are you selling a Ford Escort?'

I bloody well was. This was even better news than Steve Coogan getting in touch. Suddenly there was light at the end of the tunnel – it was possible that very soon I could look out of my window and the car wouldn't be staring back at me. I had only driven twice since the day of my journey back from Anthony's: one morning when I was late for work, and another time when Molly and I needed to go to the supermarket. But I hadn't bought the car just to carry heavy shopping. Although it was useful to fill the boot with bags of potatoes and boxes of washing powder, I didn't really feel that was the best way of getting my money's worth out of it. People like to give their cars nicknames and so I called mine the 'Cruel Mistress'. She had been a stupid thing to spend money on, but now it seemed I could be saved by a mystery caller. This man was the answer to my prayers, my Jim'll Fix It in shining armour.

'Would you like to come round and have a look?' I asked. My hand holding the phone trembled with excitement at the prospect. 'Or I could come to you?' I suggested. I was bending over backwards for him. James Lewis would be proud of me. I gave the caller my address and he told me he'd be around later that day. Back at my house I picked up my car keys and opened up the Cruel Mistress to clear her out. I wanted her to be immaculate. I even opened up the glove box I had sworn never to open again. I held my breath as I released the latch, and scooped everything into a bin bag like I was getting rid of murder evidence. I double knotted the bag and dropped it inside the wheelie bin. I took indoors my A–Z of Norwich, a box of books from the boot and my mix tape. I vacuumed out the back seat, sucking up remnants of crisps and biscuits from its previous incarnation belonging to Anthony. I knew it wasn't my mess – I'd never even had anyone in the back seat. In the kitchen I filled a bucket with warm, soapy water and went outside to wash the car, scrub it like it had never been scrubbed before. I wanted the car to look perfect. Molly and I had received a big water bill through the post the previous morning and selling the car to this mystery caller would pay a sizeable chunk of that. I scrubbed until my hands were wrinkly and murky water trickled from the bonnet to the drain. I looked at the car and was proud of my handiwork. Content that the car was in perfect condition to sell, I locked her up, went inside and waited.

And waited.

And waited.

And eventually realized I would have to give up. My buyer hadn't shown up. I had spent the afternoon watching the sky gradually darken, listening to the clock turn, until eventually, at 10 p.m., I had to concede defeat. I ended up wasting the whole evening, I achieved nothing, had been unable to focus my mind on any one activity. I have a one-track mind and unfortunately it had been focused entirely on waiting. I had spent the whole evening peering through net curtains out at the street, checking my phone and hoping the doorbell was about to ring.

As the number had been withheld it meant I hadn't been able to call my mystery man back to find out what had happened to him. I didn't even know his name. I felt really disappointed, the euphoria of receiving the initial phone call was followed by the inevitable comedown. The car was going to be with me for ever. Even if I had it scrapped it would rebuild itself, find its way from the compactor back to the kerb outside my house.

At six the next morning, my body clock jerked me into action after days of early shifts. This was no time for snoozing, unfinished business was in the air, so I got out of bed, optimistic that today would be the day I sold the Cruel Mistress. Only once it was sold would I be able to feel I could get on with my life. I got dressed, sat on the settee and waited, but it was wishful thinking. I knew there was no chance he would come in the morning. I went to work in the afternoon slightly deflated. I had to admit it was all over, no one was going to buy my stupid car, I was going to be forced to start all over again. Maybe this guy never even intended to come round at all – a newsagent's window prankster, my nemesis; he was my Lex Luther, my Hannibal Lecter, my Terry Duckworth. I imagined I was one of many he had conned, that he had phoned other people, concealing his identity, teasing them with offers: 'I would like a man with a van', 'I am interested in hiring your caravan in Hemsby', 'I may have found your missing kitten'.

Or maybe he was just someone who changed his mind and decided not to buy a car that was falling apart. What irritated me most of all was that I should have made the same decision. When I saw the advert in the newsagent's window I should have just carried on with my day, not given it a second thought. If I hadn't turned up to Anthony's that day I wouldn't be in the predicament I was in. But at the same time I would never have heard his story about proposing and falling in love and a one-way ticket to Chicago, the rest of his life changed for ever.

As it turned out the non-arrival was a blessing in disguise. That afternoon I decided I would drive to work. As I still owned the car I might as well make the most of it, put some miles on the clock. And on the way to work that afternoon something clicked inside me. For the first time since I'd bought the car I didn't feel guilty about owning it. I wound down the window, turned the radio on full blast. Somehow, I was starting to enjoy myself.

I drove to work all week. Jangling the car keys in the pocket of my work trousers made me feel a welcome sense of independence. It felt like I had discovered something new. Walking to work in the summer is fine, but six o'clock on a winter morning can be cold and unforgiving. Cycling in the rain, splashing through puddles, wearing a high-vis jacket is less rewarding than driving in a car, the heater blowing warm air in your face. After a week of parking in the hotel car park I felt almost as passionate about being behind the steering wheel as Anthony had been. Perhaps it wasn't so bad after all that the car was likely to be mine for the foreseeable future. Maybe the Cruel Mistress wasn't so cruel after all. A handy mistress. A speedy mistress. An economical mistress with plenty of gas in the tank.

The next day I was off work and so decided to go for a drive. Now that I was a driver I had a whole new world open to me, I wasn't restricted to Norwich. I could go to nearby towns and look at their newsagents' windows. I got out of bed, got dressed, jumped in the car, pushed my mix tape in the tape deck and set off with no destination in mind. At the junction at the end of my road, as I waited for a gap in the traffic, I didn't know whether I was going to turn left or right. I was enjoying the arbitrary nature of the journey, although the surrounding lanes of traffic and pedestrians didn't seem to appreciate such ambiguity. I saw a road sign for Sheringham, a seaside town about thirty miles from Norwich. I had never been there before, the sun was out and it seemed as good a place as any, so I indicated left and headed to the seaside. I wound down the window, turned the music up and a smile beamed across my face as I sang along to the mix tape I had made specially.

I had been put off driving by my first instructor when I was eighteen. He terrified me, he looked a bit like Rab C. Nesbitt and had only recently moved to the area, having lived in the East End of London for forty years. I started to dread my weekly lesson, and hearing him tooting his horn in his Renault Clio outside my house felt like a punch to the stomach. During one lesson the traffic lights turned red, so I braked (he had taught me that much), but he felt that the car behind us was, to paraphrase, 'right up our arse'.

'What a dickhead,' my instructor said, and swivelled round in his seat, waited until he had the attention of the driver and waved his middle finger at him like a windscreen wiper. In my rear-view mirror I watched as the driver got out of his car, slammed the door shut and approached our car.

'Lock your door,' my instructor said to me, unfazed. 'Last time this happened, a guy punched the kid in the driving seat,' he added without a flicker of jest. I locked my door. Luckily, the driver of the car behind recognized the antagonist in the situation and went straight to the passenger window. My instructor wound his window down slightly, for dialogue, not enough for a fist.

'What the hell's your problem?' the man shouted at him. The lights had turned to green, but I was frozen still, I didn't know whether I should drive or stay where I was, or if I should just get out of the car and walk back home, let the two of them get on with whatever was about to happen. Before the argument between my instructor and the increasingly irate man had time to escalate, my instructor noticed the traffic lights had turned to green and, like a getaway driver, I was urged to drive. It turned out to be my last lesson with him. I arranged to have a new driving instructor the following week and passed my test first time a couple of months later. Whether as a direct result of my instructor's unusual techniques, driving was never something I found enjoyable.

But everything had changed, I now realized I could enjoy it. My Road to Damascus moment was on the road to Sheringham, my foot on the accelerator pedal, the road clear in front of me, the Pixies on the stereo. I was in the driving seat.

Immediately I went in pursuit of newsagents' windows. The first newsagent was in the town centre, a wall filled with handwritten cards. You can tell a lot about an area by the content of their newsagents' windows. This window advertised a Fairtrade market, a community beach clean organized by Sheringham in Bloom, bicycles for hire at £9 a day. The content of its windows was much more aquatic than the newsagents' windows in Norwich; instead of vans and cars people were advertising sailing holidays and boat repair services, or selling boats. There was no way I was going to buy a boat. I was pretty sure there was no way I was going to buy a boat.

There were notable consistencies with newsagents' windows in Norwich. One was the plethora of adverts for lost cats and dogs, often in a child's handwriting. I also saw that Sheringham, just like Unthank Road, was having to battle against Tesco's plans to build a new store. It seemed the company was desperate to conquer East Anglia. Just as in Norwich, there were big Say No stickers, and all the shop windows displayed anti-Tesco signs. The people of Sheringham seemed passionately opposed to the building of a new store. I could imagine shopkeepers standing in front of the trucks carrying Tesco's bricks and mortar, the butchers with meat-spattered aprons waving their cleavers, the bakers with their rolling pins and clenched fists, the newsagents with their rolled-up newspapers, all stood arm in arm, singing protest songs, making sure the lorries retreated and the supermarket would never be built.

Sheringham had been a good choice of destination to spend a day away from work. I felt a bit like I was on holiday. The town seemed safe, friendly, and far removed from city life. The closest thing to a hoodie I saw was a fisherman wearing a sou'wester. It was April and a bit grey but despite this I was in a good mood. I walked away from the town centre, through stone-walled country lanes and visited a second newsagent's, which again had a huge window display, including what was possibly the most unappealing advert I had ever seen in a newsagent's window, which is quite a boast for a market dominated by loft insulations and gravel delivery services: 'For Sale, 3 Westlife tickets, £80 each.'

But one advert really interested me.

Wanted: lodger in large detached house.

21

A HOUSE IN SHERINGHAM

'Hello, I'm phoning about the room to let,' I explained to the man who answered.

He told me he was letting two rooms and both were still available. The house was a few minutes from the town centre, and he'd be back from work at five, and I'd be welcome to go round any time that evening to have a look. I scribbled down his directions and contemplated what to do, with a full five hours to idle away in Sheringham.

I've always wanted to live by the seaside. When I was little we'd go on family holidays to Whitby or Scarborough and I loved it. I never envied my friends who went to Euro Disney or Florida or beaches in Spain – for some reason I was happier closer to home. The day before my sister and I were due to get our A Level results we were really worried, so my dad drove us to Robin Hood's Bay and we spent the day on the beach. I had already resigned myself to failing my exams. I'd spent the whole summer worrying about it. But walking along the beach, I realized it didn't really matter what my results were, or whether

I went to university. No matter what happened, everything would be OK. It was the first time I had been at ease with myself for weeks. If it all went wrong I knew I could always live by the seaside. It wasn't so much the bright sunshine and yellow beaches that I was attracted to, it was glum, miserable mornings like this. There is something melancholic about an out-of-season seaside town: the sound of drizzle patting against the wet sand, the pastel colours of the sea, pensioners in raincoats. I expected to see Alan Bennett sobbing into a rock pool, Morrissey failing to win a prize in the amusement arcade.

Perhaps I was slightly too young to uproot to the coast. I'd had it in mind I would be in my dotage when I made my retreat to the seaside, a retirement plan rather than something I'd do a couple of years after graduating. But I did have to think about what I was doing next. I liked living with Molly and we both loved our house and garden, our local pub and neighbours. But I was very aware that at any moment she could announce she was moving out, that it was time to get on with her life and settle down. She had higher ambitions than drinking cups of tea and watching Pete's videos with me. If Molly did move out then I would be in the tricky position of finding somewhere new – it had been difficult enough the first time. So this was my contingency plan. It didn't mean I was going to start a new life in Sheringham straight away, that I would arrive back in Norwich that night, pack my bags and post my key through the letterbox before driving away, but it would do no harm to have a look. There wasn't much tying me to Norwich, my job was nothing special, and although I had good friends, perhaps it would do me good to relocate to the seaside, play on the slot machines, have my hair ruffled by the sea breeze. I wouldn't even have to work in Sheringham; with my car I could keep my job at the hotel in Norwich, or start somewhere else, anywhere within a few miles. This could be a chance to dip my toes in the water.

I walked down the high street, past the chip shop, the model railway shop and the boutique selling home-made fudge and realized Sheringham was the type of town you rarely see any more, a dying breed, exactly the type of place that didn't need a big supermarket.

The sun was out, the morning's rain had stopped and, deciding it was warm enough to spend time outdoors, I walked to the beach. A few people had had the same idea: a man who looked like Uncle Albert in *Only Fools and Horses* stood leaning against a wall, watching the tide coming in, the waves crashing against the shore; families picnicked on the rocks; two little girls built a castle in the sand with a bucket and spade. The cliché tells you that the vastness of the sea and sky, the trawler on the horizon, reminds us how insignificant we all are. But I looked around and saw a boy licking a piece of ice cream dripping from his cone, two old ladies sharing a tray of chips and mushy peas and it made me think the opposite, it made me feel how significant people are, getting on with their lives, making the best of things. I walked to a charity shop and found a battered, dog-eared copy of *Tom Brown's Schooldays* for 25p and sat down on the beach to read it. It felt good to be on the beach, shoes and socks taken off, reading. The seaside is so relaxing, away from the confined spaces of daily life – cashpoints and elevators, supermarket queues and offices.

After an hour of reading *Tom Brown's Schooldays* the sun disappeared behind the clouds, and it started to get too chilly to stay on the beach. Everyone who had been out when it was sunny had all left, apart from one family, who were braving it out with a picnic, stubbornly wrapped in jumpers and coats, refusing to let the weather interfere with their day. It was when I noticed I had goosebumps that I decided it was time to go inside, so went to the Lobster, a pub that advertised fresh crab on its blackboard outside. Crab is a speciality in these parts. Cromer, famous across the world for its crabs, is just up the road, and it didn't seem right to eat anything other than fresh local seafood. I ordered, and as I gave the barmaid my order the stereo started playing Otis Redding's 'Sittin' on the Dock of the Bay'. Someone must have realized a visitor was in town and got out the coastal hits tape. I expected that as I tucked into my crab I'd be treated to 'We're all going on a summer holiday . . .'

At half past five I made my way to the house, and I thought about how I'd feel if the situation was different, if I was going with a genuine intention of moving in. The house was on an estate a few minutes away from the peace and quiet of Sheringham centre. I found the right road – a cul-de-sac near a busy road, and the novelty of the sandcastles and seagulls started to disappear, and, like a road in any town in the country, it didn't feel so special any more.

Steve answered the door, a short, stocky man a few years older than me, with a laminated name badge dangling from a lanyard. He had rosy red cheeks, short curly hair and a welcoming smile.

'John?' he asked. I nodded and he let me in.

'I better take my shoes off,' I said. They were damp as a result of misjudging a wave when I walked along the shore.

'It doesn't matter,' Steve said, shrugging his shoulders, so I kept them on. I followed my potential landlord along the hallway and he opened a door.

'This is the kitchen,' he said, but hesitated, not really knowing what to say about it, realizing the lack of narrative in a small room. 'Big fridge,' he said, pointing at a big fridge. 'Microwave,' he said, pointing at a microwave. I followed him through to the utility room. 'All mod cons,' he said, which is Latin for 'lots of electrical equipment'.

The kitchen was in dire need of Domestos; the surfaces were grimy, but it was the layer of melted cheese at the bottom of the oven, the mould on the skirting board that made me want to sterilize things. I am not an overly tidy person. I have lived with neurotic people and driven them crazy with my piles of dirty pots in the sink, a reluctance to hoover and a seeming inability to take my shoes off before traipsing mud over carpets, but the house left me with an unsettling feeling.

The living room was clearly a different matter, and he seemed much more interested in showing it to me.

'Come through,' he said, like a little kid showing off his treehouse. The room was immaculate, with a huge blue rug on the floor and two red leather settees. In one corner stood lava lamps, opposite those was a huge television set, games consoles and a stack of computer games.

'We've got Sky and Nintendo Wii.' He pointed at the television tangle of controllers. 'And there's more through here,' he said, opening up a set of French doors to reveal a conservatory, with patio furniture, pot plants and another television set. In my head I decided that this second room would be where I would spend most of my time. It's where I'd store my books and records and stereo. This would be my living room, Steve could have the other room. I had it all planned out.

'You'd be free to use this room as much as you wanted,' he said. I nodded, and was starting to feel I would be perfectly comfortable living there. He went on, 'I'm letting out two bedrooms . . . a girl, Bella, came round last night and said she would probably take the upstairs one, so it's most likely you'll be downstairs. Is that OK?'

I nodded, and we went through to look at what could be my future bedroom.

'I bought this house a couple of years ago and lived here with my mate, but he moved out a couple of weeks ago. He's still not been back for his stuff, but obviously if you wanted the room I would make sure he came to get it.'

There was no bed, no wardrobe, instead there was a tennis racket and lots of rucksacks. There was no way I could move into another unfurnished house. I didn't have the best track record when it came to that.

'Would I have to furnish the bedroom myself?' I asked.

'I'm afraid so.'

I was a little disappointed, temporarily forgetting that as I wasn't going to move into the house anyway it didn't matter.

'Would that be a problem?' he asked. 'Is being downstairs a problem?'

'No, it's fine. It's a good-size room.'

Steve took me upstairs to show me the peripherals of the rest of the house: his bedroom, the room that would belong to the other lodger, and the airing cupboard. The upstairs tour took perhaps three seconds, with just enough time for me to stick my head into each room and nod approvingly.

'Shall we go through to the living room and I'll tell you about the rent?' he suggested, and we went downstairs, hopefully without me traipsing too many dirty marks over his clean light carpets.

'Do you want a cup of tea?' he asked. I nodded, and made myself comfortable on one of the settees to admire his DVD collection as he put the kettle on. Like Pete's videos, the preference seemed to be towards horror, such as *Saw* and *Hostel*. But what endeared me even more towards Steve, who I already sensed I could quite happily live with, was that he had *Home Alone* on DVD. It's hard to dislike someone who owns *Home Alone*.

'It's a great house, and doesn't cost much. It's near a couple of pubs, they're both pretty cheap, really friendly,' Steve said once we had mugs of tea in our hands. 'My mate moved in, but a couple of months ago he told me he was moving in with his missus.' He blew into his mug. 'Where do you live now?' he asked, perhaps not wanting to dwell on being ditched by his mate.

'Norwich. But I might have to move out of my house,' I said, a somewhat elaborate version of the truth. 'And I was in Sheringham earlier this afternoon and saw your advert in a newsagent's window.'

'Aah, that's right.'

'Have the rooms been advertised for long?'

'Not at all, I put up adverts here on Monday and a couple more in newsagents in other towns nearby yesterday, and it's in the newspaper too. This is my second response in . . . three days, you and Bella.'

'So do you think she will move in?'

'Yeah, I'm pretty sure she will. I kind of know her, she knows some of my mates. Everyone in Sheringham knows each other. I've lived here since I was six months old and can't go into town without waving and saying hello to people I know. It wouldn't take long until it was like that for you.'

I liked that idea.

'What's it like here then? I've always wondered what it would be like to live in a seaside town.'

Steve assessed the question, cocking his head from side to side.

'In the summer it's OK. It gets very busy, thousands of tourists, which is a bit annoying because you can never find a parking space. But in the winter it's bleak. *So* bleak.' He blew on his tea again and shook his head. 'It's just empty, deserted. You'll go to town on a Sunday to buy some milk and there's just no one about. You get used to it though, it's just a bit strange some-times.' He moved his stare up from the floor and looked at me again. 'I must like it though,' he said, suddenly positive, 'because I've never moved away and decided to buy a house here.'

He talked me through bills and rent, the house was incredibly cheap – a month's rent and bills was much cheaper than what I was paying in Norwich. And I'd get to have Sky TV, a Wii and *Home Alone* on DVD. But despite the extra disposable income I knew how much I didn't want to be a lodger. I've been a lodger before, when I lived in Germany, and didn't enjoy it much, craved the chance to move out. It's impossible to shake the feeling that you're living in someone else's home, that you are a guest rather than a resident. It made me realize how much I enjoyed living with Molly.

'I'd better get going,' I said to Steve. 'I should let you get on with things.' I made a move to put my coat on.

'Yeah, I do have to go to work in an hour,' he said, checking the time on his watch.

'Can I let you know in a couple of days what I decide?'

'Yes, of course, take your time. If anyone else seems interested I'll let you know so we can move things as quickly as possible.'

I opened the front door, thanked Steve for his time and took one last look around the house.

'I'll see you later,' I said somewhat optimistically, and as I walked away, past people who would have been my neighbours, I thought that for all Steve knew he was going to spend the next couple of years with me. We shared an interest in football and cricket, but that wasn't enough. Meeting Steve affected me more than I thought it would. My car was parked at the train station, but I wasn't ready to drive back to Norwich just yet. I wanted to spend more time by the seaside. The sun was setting over the Norfolk coast, so I walked back to the beach.

I thought about what I'd just seen. If I hadn't been so settled where I was, I would probably have been interested. Steve had a pretty straightforward life – work, Norwich City, a big telly. But when I met Pete in his bedsit to buy the videos it wasn't the squalor or grime that worried me, it was the isolation. I had the exact same twinge of sadness when I was with Steve, whose home was spacious, well furnished. It was the lack of someone to talk to about your day, to share things with, to spend time with. I realized how little I wanted to live like that, how much I valued living with someone. What if I got a call one day to say something had happened to someone in my family, someone I was close to. I wouldn't be able to deal with it if I lived with Steve. I couldn't talk things through with him. I worried about having no one close to me.

I left the beach, walked back to my car. I liked Sheringham a lot, the tearooms and fishing boats, chip butties, and families on the beach pouring pre-mixed bottles of orange squash into plastic cups. I wasn't ready to settle down. The freedom of driving in my car had reminded me how much I thrive on my independence. I didn't want to move to Sheringham. I was happy in Norwich. I wasn't sure how long I would stick around, I still felt the urge to go back to Germany, and back to Vienna. But I was fairly sure I wouldn't go through with it. I sensed I'd be in Norwich for the foreseeable future, and maybe that would be fine. In my head I could justify what I had done, I had responded to Steve's advert and satisfied my curiosity. But as I drove away from Sheringham I hoped I hadn't wasted his time. He was a nice bloke, and I felt a bit bad at leaving him there, home alone.

22

MARTINS THE NEWSAGENT

The sea air and long walk along the beach meant I enjoyed a refreshing, deep night's sleep. The next morning I woke up feeling a renewed sense of optimism about the future, that the sanctuary of Sheringham had given me a sense of clarity. I texted Steve to tell him I wouldn't be moving in with him. He texted back and seemed disappointed, wanting to make sure there hadn't been anything in particular about the house I'd disliked. I replied, reassuring him I'd have been happy there, it was just that I was staying in Norwich. I hoped Bella hadn't let him down too, and was sure newsagents' windows would help him as much as they had helped me.

A couple of minutes later my phone starting ringing, again an unknown number, and I answered it, wondering whether it was Steve wanting to pick my brains some more.

'Hello?'

'Hi,' the voice said as I poured sand out of my shoes, 'I've just seen an advert for your car.'

This had to be it. I couldn't take rejection a second time. My customer, Ian, said he'd be round in an hour, and sixty minutes later there he was, standing on my doorstep, right on time. You could set your watch by Ian. I walked out and we stood together by the car, the morning sun blazing. A man cycled past us with no top on, his bare chest may as well have had the words *summer is here* tattooed across.

'Could I look under the bonnet?' Ian asked, and I floundered underneath the steering wheel, trying to work out how to click it open. Once the lid was released, Ian rummaged around, heaving sighs as he fiddled around with various parts of the engine. He was the dentist; the Cruel Mistress his patient with her mouth wide open.

'I don't think it's got much life left in it,' he told me.

I didn't trust Ian. He wore a tatty anorak, a Guinness T-shirt and lime-green tracksuit bottoms. He shook his head and raised his eyebrows. 'It doesn't look great,' he said, his tone all matter-of-fact as he adjusted his silver-rimmed spectacles.

Either Ian knew a lot about cars, or he was trying to pull off a good deal, full of chutzpah on my own doorstep. I was suspicious that he was trying to con me and he thought he could get away with it. That could have been the case before my trip to Sheringham, but I had started to enjoy having the car, I wasn't going to just give it away. I bought it out of politeness, I wasn't going to sell it out of politeness too. I was prepared to fight my corner.

'It seems to be in pretty good condition to me,' I told him. 'I drive it every day and never have a problem.'

'It's got a year, max.' Ian's hands were smudged with diesel oil which he wiped on his tracksuit bottoms.

'I think it's got more than that,' I told him. 'There's a good few years left.'

Ian shook his head again. 'I'm a mechanic, I've worked with cars for more than twenty years. I've got a few parts in my garage I might be able to use. Fix it up, prolong its life for maybe eighteen months.'

It was starting to look like the car was going to be staying with me a little longer. Ian was winning, it was obvious I knew nothing about cars, he'd seen the way I fumbled to get the bonnet open. I had really thought this might be my chance to get rid of the car. I wasn't desperate, but if I could make as much of my money back as possible my life would be so much easier.

'Do you think you'll be making an offer?' I asked, trying to hurry along proceedings and go back inside, deal or no deal.

'I won't be able to give you much at all,' he said. I had anticipated this. 'I can take it off your hands for twenty quid?'

I hadn't anticipated this. Twenty quid! I checked to see whether this was a wind-up, but I could detect no smirk, no wry smile. This was for real.

'Twenty pounds?'

'Yeah. It's not got many more miles in it,' he repeated.

I was getting fed up. It was only a few months earlier that I had paid £280 for it. Maybe that had been far too much. Maybe even the £200 I had initially offered had been too high a price. When I spent time with Anthony it made me feel uncomfortable, but with Ian I felt even worse. I was out of my depth in the motor industry. I was surrounded by people taking the piss.

'Twenty pounds is a lot less than it was advertised for,' I told him. It was difficult to stay deadpan, the conversation had taken such a surreal slant. I couldn't bring myself to suggest a figure I'd be prepared to sell it for. When I wrote out the card and placed it in the newsagent's window I had expected that there might be a certain amount of leeway – this was a difference in opinion of £260. Even meeting Ian halfway would have left me considerably short-changed.

'There's more than twenty quids' worth of petrol in there!' I said, exasperated, getting annoyed at Ian's obvious unwillingness to increase his offer. I wanted him to leave. I didn't want him anywhere near my house or my car. He was wasting my time, we both knew there was going to be no deal.

'You'll regret it if you say no,' he said. 'You'll end up paying to get it scrapped.' We said goodbye, Ian walked away from my house and I went back inside, both of us shaking our heads, both of our mornings wasted. As I made my way upstairs I tried to work out whether I had made the right decision.

Once again I felt frustrated at owning the car. The two of us were destined to grow old together. We'd be taking each other to garden centres on bank holiday afternoons before too long. I had enjoyed driving around, and my attitude towards the Cruel Mistress had improved considerably since my trip to Sheringham. I had discovered the enjoyment of driving; there is something special about man bonding with Ford Escort and mix tape. It is a way to be by yourself, doors locked, able to go wherever you choose. I started to understand why Anthony had devoted so much of his life to driving, and wondered whether by now he was in a Lincoln Continental, cruising down the highways, his kids in the back seat, whooping with delight. I hoped so, anyway.

But being in a car was fun. I wondered whether I should leave the hotel trade and start a new career as a cabbie. Maybe I should buy a van, travel the country picking up hitchhikers, spend night after night in the middle lane of the motorway, stopping off for early-morning fry-ups. Perhaps before too long I would even be able to feel I had got my money's worth out of the Cruel Mistress. Suddenly everywhere was accessible. On my next day off work I went to a party. When I saw on Facebook that one of my friends in Lincoln was having a party, it would normally have been useless information. But that afternoon I threw a bag in the back of the car and a few hours later I was at the party. The next day I drove to my mum and dad's to say hello, then a few weeks later I drove to Manchester to go out for someone's birthday. All of these things would have been unlikely without a car. It was like discovering a magic carpet. And whenever I went somewhere new I would make sure I looked at newsagents' windows. I loved driving through the night, singing along to my tapes, or listening to phone-ins on late-night talk radio. Massage Lucy had told me to find a way to relax, and I had stumbled across my way of doing so by accident; cruising country lanes in my Escort at midnight.

I decided to set off on a road trip, and it was when I was in town looking at the window of Martins the Newsagent that I found something I could do. Martins is the indisputable king of newsagents' windows. Despite being a huge chain of 900 stores, Martins maintains an incredible community-based focus. Whereas most chains cover their windows with in-store advertising and special offers, you can barely see through the glass of Martins stores for all the postcards advertising Get Rich Quick schemes, Indian head massages, Ford Sierras and babysitters available.

I feel very affectionate towards Martins. It's the store I did a paper round for, diligently biking round town after school every day for three years, shoving the *Scunthorpe Evening Telegraph* through letterboxes. As soon as my newsagent's window life started to gain speed, Martins had been my 'go to' guy for bits and pieces. Their windows sprawl like Spitalfields Market, with so many goods for sale, anything you could ever want: a roof rack for a Vauxhall Astra, a second-hand piano or a Polish girl to do your ironing. If you need your clutch repaired or want to buy a second-hand nest of tables you will almost certainly find somewhere in a Martins window. I decided to set out on a one-day holiday, visiting every Martins the Newsagent in the Yellow Pages. It was hardly an odyssey on the scale of Homer or Gorman, but I thought it would be interesting to see what I could find.

Martins was founded in 1901 by a former footballer, Robert Smyth of Glasgow. In fact Smyth's story was incredibly similar to Norwich's Alan Taylor – not only were they both retired foot-ballers who opened up stores, but they had both been strikers, and prolific goal-scorers, Taylor's two FA Cup Final goals matched by Smyth's twelve goals in twelve games for Scotland. A pattern was emerging and I couldn't understand why Robbie Fowler and Les Ferdinand had never opened their own newsagents.

The first Martins on my list was North Walsham, a fifteen-mile drive halfway between Norwich and Sheringham. I made an early start so I could cram in every Martins on my list. It was 6 a.m. and the early-morning sea mist hovered over the deserted country lanes as I drove coastwards. I arrived in North Walsham, found a parking space in Lidl's car park and then shortly afterwards rediscovered the ability to position a car between two white lines. Satisfied with my half-parked, half-abandoned car, I walked through the marketplace, eagerly anticipating Martins. North Walsham is pretty, a quintessential market town seemingly undamaged by the twenty-first century, with fruit shops and chemists and dads walking their kids to school, a backpack on each shoulder. Martins was one of the few chain stores in the town. The huge closed-down Woolworth's with blacked-out windows had clearly once been the hub of North Walsham's shopping activity – and now mums and dads would have to find new places to buy school uniforms, and toys at Christmas. The Martins window was generous with its adverts, and at £1 a week must have meant they were turning over around £200 a month just through their window services. The window painted a portrait of the town, a Besson cornet for £55, dachshund puppies for £750, a Seat Ibiza for £1,200. It told a story of a middle England town, unused musical instruments and expensive family pets. For breakfast I went to the fruit shop. I looked around at carrots with their leafy tops and potatoes swimming in soil, and fresh fruit that looked like it had been picked from a tropical island.

I left North Walsham and drove to Lowestoft, a few miles away, where I ate a bacon baguette, drank hot chocolate and did Kakuro in the *Guardian* while the good people of the town got on with their lives. The newsagents' windows there had more adverts for boats, for Indian head massages, a camper van for £3,000, a fully automated blood pressure monitor. I didn't stay for long. After Lowestoft I went to Attleborough, and by the afternoon I had visited seven Martins. It was one of the best days I'd had for a long time, completely at ease as I travelled through the villages of East Anglia. I used to assume that sitting in a cafe or a pub with a drink and a book or the newspaper was something you would have to be a long way from home to do. It is something I did regularly when I lived abroad. But now, even though I was only twenty minutes from my house, I felt as if I was on my holidays. My mobile phone was at home, I knew I wasn't going to bump into someone I knew, it was just me, and I knew I was not going to be disturbed. Some people go to Bangladesh, Taiwan, Mumbai to discover themselves. I'm happier close to home, in Sheringham, Diss, Bungay. I find travelling less stressful when you know you can go home and have a bath. I can't go to the Pacific like Michael Palin. I can't ride a motorbike from Mongolia to New York like Ewan McGregor or get my kicks on Route 66. I had a job. I had no money. I'd probably get travel sick.

The final Martins I drove to was Bowthorpe, a small industrial Norfolk town that wouldn't get into any of the local tourist brochures. I switched on the car radio, tuned in to a local station and was immediately hit by bad news. Tesco had been given the go-ahead to build their new store in Unthank Road. The pro-testers had lost. I was much more annoyed than I thought I would be and became convinced it was all a conspiracy, that the result had been inevitable all along. It was appropriate that it was in Bowthorpe that I discovered the bad news; I had bad associ-ations with Bowthorpe.

The only other time I had been there was in my second year of university, when my housemate Mark and I cycled two and a half miles in the rain to play football. We lost 18–0 and then had to bike all the way home, aching and beaten. The journey back was miserable and humiliating, although probably worse for Mark. He had been in goal. However, the promise of more newsagents being there for me, particularly Martins in the shopping centre meant that it was worth reliving these painful memories.

Even so, it was in Bowthorpe where things took a turn for the worse. I parked, walked around the shopping centre, wrote down in my notebook things I'd found interesting in Martins window, much more prosaic than Lowestoft or Sheringham – have your car towed for free, two propane gas cylinders for £25, grass-cutting services. I returned to my car, put my key into the lock but it did not open. Nothing clicked, nothing twisted, there was no kerchunk. I tried again. I twisted the key round and round, I twizzled, I forced and I swore but the lock had broken. There was no way I could get it open. This must be what had happened to the passenger's side too. I took the keys out and surveyed my options. The sunroof and all the windows were closed. I realized I had never noticed there was a sunroof. The discovery wasn't enough to comfort me. I went round to the boot; if I could open this I could crawl inside and everything would be OK. I put the key in and twisted it. Everything hinged on this. But nothing happened. I twisted it the other way. Failure. I was locked out. I wiggled the keys again and again, resorting to brute strength, or at least as close to brute strength as I can muster. I was red-in-the-face angry. Angry at being stranded, angry at the inevitable cost this was going to lead to, angry because I had lots of tapes in the glove compartment, my glasses on the dashboard, my copy of *Tom Brown's Schooldays* on the back seat. How could they be taken from me so cruelly?

When I took the key out of the lock it was bent out of shape. It no longer resembled a key, just as my journey home no longer resembled a comfortable drive while listening to Simon Mayo on the car radio.

I am not a resourceful person. At times I can be an intensely useless person. I didn't have my mobile phone because I was trying to be bohemian. Luckily, Directory Enquiries exists to be resourceful on behalf of people like me, so I went to a phone box and gave them a call. The woman from Directory Enquiries was so helpful that I half expected her to fix the car herself. I didn't know who I needed to speak to, whether I needed a garage or a mechanic or a towing company. I explained my problem and was sympathetically put through to the Ford garage in Norwich.

After putting me on hold the woman at Ford told me there was nothing she could do. To have it towed away would cost £150, and that was before the cost of repair. I reluctantly ended my conversation with her with no solution. I was not part of any breakdown service, or if I was all the documents were in the folder that I'd been given when I bought the car, which lay underneath the passenger's seat, and there was no way I could afford to pay £150. All the money in my bank account had been swallowed up by the car, including a six-month tax disc which I had bought a week earlier and a full tank of petrol paid for that morning. I was being punished for my exuberance. I should have stayed at home watching Pete's videos.

I took a moment to take a step back and assess the situation. I was locked out and too far from home to walk back. I glared at the car for long enough for it to know it had done something wrong. But then I remembered one of the adverts in the Martins window. I walked back to the newsagent to have a proper look.

We tow away unwanted cars.

This could be my chance to put an end to things, to put both me and the Cruel Mistress out of our misery once and for all. I didn't need to think twice, I walked to a phone box, filled the slot with loose change before calling the number and explaining my predicament.

A man called Brendan, who owned a recovery company, told me he'd come to help me.

In Bowthorpe shopping centre there was a cafe but I decided to wait by my car. I didn't deserve coffee and scones. I would pace up and down by my car until the Cruel Mistress was gone for ever.

'Would you rather I tried to fix it or just scrap it?' Brendan asked. He had brought his mate with him and they had arrived towing a huge trailer. It was quite a sight as it arrived through the car park entrance, the scale of the vehicle making me realize what I had done. I had caused a mess and had needed to call a man to sort it out for me.

I really wasn't sure what I wanted. Scrapping it would be an end to my problems, but I baulked at the thought of the money I had wasted, and was clinging on to the romantic image of me driving along the country lanes after work. I had only just learned to appreciate the benefits the car could offer me. I looked at the trailer, and Brendan and his mate. It made me sad to think of the car being scrapped. It had done bad things but it wasn't the car's fault. It was being punished for my own mistakes. Maybe it deserved a second chance.

'Do you think you could fix it?' I asked, knowing I may live to regret it.

Brendan lifted a toolbox out from his passenger seat, took my car key and managed to open the door. His arms were so much wider than mine, and he opened the door with ease. I felt useless, that I was a little boy who needed his dad to help him out. He tried the engine, which purred perfectly.

'You'll have to be very careful when you lock and unlock your door,' he said, 'but other than that the car's fine.'

'So it's OK to drive?'

'It's fine, mate. It's up to you. It'll be expensive to fix the locks, but if you're careful it'll be OK. The engine's fine.'

I had a decision to make. This wasn't my biggest strength; poor decision-making is what had got me into this problem in the first place.

'I'm going to keep it,' I told him. I feared I would rue such decisiveness, but I didn't want to lose the car this way.

'No probs,' Brendan said. 'If you do need it scrapped at any stage give me a call.' He handed me his business card. I paid him his call-out fee and got back in the car to drive it home. There would be no more midnight drives. No more driving to work. I parked outside my house, but didn't lock the door. I wasn't going to be naive enough to do that again. I didn't need to worry about it being stolen. This car was clearly destined to be with me for ever.

23

THE WRESTLING MATCH

A letter came in the post marked NHS. It reminded me about my second appointment for a blood donation. The letter revealed that my blood type was B positive, which sounds like the motto Massage Lucy had instilled in me. I looked B positive up online, and found out it was one of the rarer groups. Only 7 per cent of the population have the same blood type as me, which included Paul McCartney. Which means that if ever he's in need of an urgent donation, I would be able to roll up my sleeve and give him some of my rare, precious blood.

My appointment was for Easter Sunday. This time the venue was the Norwich Assembly Rooms, and I was much more relaxed after my experiences the first time round.

'So you have B positive blood,' my nurse said to me, looking through my forms.

'That's rare, isn't it?' I asked, already aware of the answer.

'That's right,' she said. 'I have very average, common blood. But that means it's more useful because more people need it.'

Already I felt deflated. I hadn't thought of it that way; my blood was useless to 93 per cent of the population. I might as well have stayed at home. Soon though it was time to lie down on a bed; my arm was tapped in search of a good juicy vein, and I lay back and looked forward to my squash.

The nurse was chatty, and as I gave blood I lay in awe at the jobs some people do. This time giving blood was as painless as buying shoelaces.

'Try not to do anything too strenuous for the rest of the day,' my nurse said as she applied the plaster and I swung my legs back to the floor. A restful evening wasn't likely though, I had something special planned for the evening. I had seen an advert in a newsagent's window that said

Easter Sunday, The Talk presents
World Association Wrestling Championships,
Erik Isaksen v The Zebra Kid.

I was going to a wrestling match. This was going to be brilliant. This was exactly the reason I was using newsagents' windows as a guide to how to spend my free time.

When I was at primary school wrestling seemed the most popular thing on the planet. But I hated everything about the World Wrestling Federation – Hulk Hogan, the Undertaker and Brett the Hitman Hart. Wrestling was the only thing the other boys would talk about; they would play with their wrestling figures, eat sandwiches from their Macho Man Randy Savage lunchboxes, imitate fight moves at playtime. Everyone in the playground was obsessed with it, but I couldn't watch it because my mum and dad didn't love me enough to install Sky

TV in our house. They didn't care about new episodes of *The Simpsons*, or being able to watch music channels all day long. Because of this neglect, I was left out of conversations in the school canteen just because I didn't know anything about wrestling. Gradually, I managed to pick up names and terminology; it was so popular it was impossible not to. I knew there was a wrestler called Jake the Snake who carried a python around his neck. And I knew that a clothesline was when you stretched out your arm and ran into someone, knocking them over. But it wasn't enough, and meant I felt as alienated then as I do now when my friends talk about business conferences, honeymoons and home births.

But now I was going to a wrestling match. I was doing it for my eight-year-old self, who was sat in the school canteen wishing he had Sky TV or a Jake the Snake lunchbox. It was nothing like the glamour of the World Wrestling Federation in the 1980s. The WAW or World Association of Wrestling was founded by husband and wife wrestlers who have also run pubs in Norwich. The venue for the night was a room in a pub in Norwich, and had as much glamour as two blokes fighting in a car park.

When I got home after reading the advert I typed Erik Isaksen and the Zebra Kid into YouTube. But what I saw was terrifying. The video featured two wrestlers fighting in a room smaller than my living room. There was no ring, just a roped-off section of a pub, and an audience of ten people sitting on chairs close to the action, liable at any moment to be knocked off by a stray wrestler. I was scared by how intimate it seemed, how close the audience were to what was going on. I could imagine being taken into the ring in a headlock, in the arms of a sweaty Norwegian wrestler, the crowd baying for my blood. I'd been worried enough about sitting in the front row for an Alan Ayckbourn play. An event with violence at its core was not my ideal way of spending an evening. Particularly not on Easter Sunday. But I was still determined to go; somehow the paradox of religious holiday and wrestling seemed irresistible. But as I was slightly taken aback by the nature of the YouTube video, I thought it best to phone the venue to check it would be OK before I actually booked a ticket. I asked whether the wrestling would be suitable for a twelve-year-old. I worked out I had approximately the same level of bravery as a twelve-year-old boy, so if they told me it wouldn't be suitable for this fictional small child then it certainly wouldn't be suitable for me.

'It's fine for children,' the lady on the phone told me, 'as long as they are accompanied by a grown-up.'

'OK, I'll make sure he's accompanied,' I told her, and wrote *wrestling* in my diary. I walked through to Molly's room.

'Do you want to go to a wrestling match?'

Molly's fee was a Smarties Easter Egg, which we scoffed cross-legged on the living-room floor while getting excited about the evening ahead. I hadn't told Molly about the YouTube video and about how scary I thought it was going to be. I would let her find out the hard way.

'What do you wear to go wrestling?' Molly shouted into my room, when it was already time to go. I worried that she might come through wearing a giant foam finger. When we were both ready we wiped the chocolate from our mouths and set off, both of us feeling a bit sick, Molly because of overindulgence in Smarties, me through pure terror. We walked to the pub to meet our friend Andy, who was lending me his camera for photographic proof to show future generations.

'I want a photo of me with my arm around a fat wrestler for my Facebook page,' Molly told us as I put the camera in my bag.

'Why are you going to wrestling?' Andy asked us. It wasn't an unreasonable question, but I didn't want to explain what I had been doing with newsagents' windows. I was preoccupied with the image of being dragged from my chair into the wrestling ring and being held aloft by a chunky man in underpants, spinning me round like a golfing umbrella while the crowd shouted 'Kill, kill, kill.'

'We thought it would be funny,' Molly explained. Andy sipped his pint and nodded. It was a good enough explanation for him. Even so, he declined our offer to come.

We finished our beers and went to The Talk, a seventies-style venue that hosted singles night every Monday and salsa dancing every Friday. We paid our tenner on the door and already two wrestlers were in the ring. The place was heaving, people were chanting, clapping. Perhaps five hundred people were crowded in the room, two cameramen were capturing everything, and there was a huge screen where we could see the action. This was nothing like I had expected. I started to relax a little. We ordered a couple of beers and the fight started. We practically had ringside seats, open-mouthed at the sight of two grown men pretending to fight ten metres in front of us.

'Hit him, you poofter,' shouted a man behind me, setting the tone for the evening, and Molly was unable to control her glee at the sight of the two wrestlers fighting as realistically as Basil and Manuel in *Fawlty Towers*. The fight lasted three minutes before the bell rang and the Tattooed Warrior, the crowd's favourite, was declared the winner, his hand held aloft by the referee.

The two wrestlers disappeared backstage but there was no time to get bored. Immediately there was a burst of entrance music – 'Jump Around' by House of Pain – and it was time for the second fight. The first wrestler arrived in the ring, a huge man who punched the air, and roared at the crowd. The master of ceremonies, a grey-haired man in a tuxedo who looked like Syd Little, introduced his opponent as the holder of the Hertfordshire and Essex British Heavyweight Championship, and he emerged to the sound of 'Let Me Entertain You' by Robbie Williams, and circled the ring on a lap of honour, high-fiving anyone in the front row he could get near, parading his title belt like he was Ali or Tyson. It was hard to take seriously. He had a physique that was more Annie Lennox than Lennox Lewis, more Mr Benn than Nigel Benn.

His opponent was, as the crowd pointed out vociferously, a fat bastard. It was only the second fight of the night and although I still felt slightly self-conscious, that couldn't be said of Molly, who was joining in with the chants. I'd never seen her so happy.

I had expected a room full of overweight men, with mullets and football shirts, and although there were people there who flaunted one or both of those accessories, I wasn't as out of place as I had feared. I certainly hadn't needed to be so concerned for my well-being, there were plenty of young kids there, joining in with Molly's songs, which would make even Millwall football supporters blush. The fat bastard retreated from the ring after being clotheslined by the hardest bloke in Hertfordshire, who shouted, 'That's the way I roll,' and the crowd screamed in delight. They changed their fat bastard chant to one of 'Chicken, chicken'. The fat bastard lost and left the ring, booed like a pantomime villain. Molly turned to me after the fight and the look in her eyes said 'This is brilliant'. We hadn't expected it would be anything like as much fun as this.

'Another drink?' she asked, and while she jostled at the bar the next fight started, a quick turnaround, the night was fervent and relentless with no time for the atmosphere to dip.

But this was a fight with a difference. The night had just got a lot more interesting.

'What's going on?' Molly asked, handing me my beer and sitting back down on our step. I tried to answer but couldn't, my jaw had dropped, and she said my face had gone a funny colour.

'It's ladies' tag teams,' Syd Little told the crowd. I had my head down, looking for the zoom function on Andy's camera. The men in the crowd were suddenly subdued, open-mouthed, love hearts in their eyes. These were wrestling, battling babes. It was not just ladies wrestling, but incredibly attractive ladies wrestling. Of the four girls in the ring, three of them looked like Cheryl Cole. Admittedly the other looked like Janice Battersby, but that's still not a bad ratio. As the babes grappled, jostled, pinned each other down you could hear a pin drop. It was like the *Nuts* magazine Christmas party.

By now I'd grown used to the simulation of wrestling. It was all incredibly well choreographed and rehearsed; the somersaults, backflips and flying kicks were really exciting to watch. But what I was most surprised about was how easily Molly and I fitted in with the crowd. We had gone to the wrestling because we thought it would be quite funny, a bit reckless. In truth we had gone to mock, to scorn. Molly had been enjoying the reactions of her friends when she updated her Facebook page with 'Molly is going to the wrestling'. It was a totally stupid thing for us to be doing, but I hadn't realized until I was actually there that our reasons were the same as everyone else that was there. We were all there for the same purpose – to have fun. And this was entertainment in its purest form; it was pantomime, theatre, cabaret. It wasn't so far removed from going to see the Alan Ayckbourn play. The wrestlers were interacting with each other in the same way as the actors at the Maddermarket Theatre played their roles, following their lines and stage directions. It was all an illusion that the audience entered into, whether at the theatre or the wrestling.

After the four girls had left the arena to raucous applause that Madonna and Girls Aloud could only dream about, the next fight was Scott Fusion versus Jimmy Ocean. The most famous figure in the history of British wrestling is Big Daddy, whose real name was Shirley Crabtree. But even that name looked positively macho in comparison to Scott Fusion and Jimmy Ocean. Why didn't these people have proper manly names like Hulk Hogan or Bruce Grobbelaar? It was the last fight before the break, during which we followed the scent of salt and vinegar and joined a queue to buy cones of chips. I went to the toilet and on my way out was stopped in my tracks by a face I recognized.

'Stew!'

'John!'

Both of us stood there, staring at each other as we digested what had just happened. We had bumped into each other at a wrestling match. It was like running into your dad at a brothel. Or worse, your mum.

'This is . . . embarrassing,' I said to him, and we both laughed. It was really good to see Stewart, and in fact, it wasn't so surprising to see him there. He only lived down the road and was a big wrestling fan. When Stewart and I lived together at university he never made any secret about how much he loved wrestling. He regularly wore a T-shirt with a picture of The Rock on it, and one afternoon we went to Toys R Us and he bought a wrestling commentator's microphone, with four different functions, which changed your voice when you held it to your mouth and commentated. Of course Stewart was going to be at the wrestling. But it must have been a bit of a shock for him to see me there. Someone who had been baffled at how a grown man could spend money on a wrestling microphone. We both stood there, not sure of what to say. I felt guilty that I hadn't seen him for at least three months, and still hadn't returned his *Curb Your Enthusiasm* DVD I'd borrowed last time I'd been round at his house.

'How come you're here?' he asked.

'I saw it advertised in a newsagent's window,' I said. 'So thought I'd come and check it out. It's amazing!' I said. The fights before the interval had been so much fun, and I was starting to understand why Stew loved wrestling so much. At university it had been an odd thing for someone to like, most of my other friends liked the Strokes and cider and sitting on the stairs at parties talking about the Smiths. But now I had entered Stew's world, things started to make sense.

'It is amazing,' he said. 'It's a really high standard tonight too.'

'After the first fight I thought it was rubbish,' I told him, 'but since then every fight has been amazing.'

'Yeah, it's one of the best I've been to.'

It was useful to have Stew as a frame of reference, to put it into a wrestling context, and that it wasn't just for novelty value that amateurs like me and Molly were enjoying it.

'Who are you talking to, Stew?' one of his mates said to him and I left him to explain to his friends who I was, while I went back to Molly to tell her about my encounter.

'Coming up, the Zebra Kid!' Syd Little said, his voice booming out of the massive speakers around the room. The crowd roared 'Zebra, Zebra' and this time I joined in; it wasn't a conscious decision, I was losing my inhibitions, and started singing along with the rest of the crowd. I started to understand the nature of mob mentality; when you are swept away, your personality is abandoned and you take on the assumed identity of the mass.

The Zebra Kid's opponent, Erik Isaksen, didn't seem to have brought many fans with him from Norway. The fight lasted several rounds and not much of it was fought in the ring, but on the floor, chasing each other around the perimeter, with chairs, beer glasses, and any weapon they could get their hands on. But by now I was familiar with proceedings, there was no violence, no contact. I realized that even in that YouTube clip I had seen no one was at risk. When the Zebra Kid threatened Erik Isaksen with a wooden stool it was as dangerous as a character in a play picking up a vase and threatening to throw it at her on-stage husband. Isaksen had his manager with him, who got the Zebra Kid in a headlock when the referee wasn't looking and the young kids sat nearby went ballistic at the facade – the baddie chasing the goodie.

'Leave him alone,' a little lad, who had a filthier vocab even than Molly, shouted at the baddies. As the fight was staged almost entirely outside the ring, members of the audience became involved; it was getting difficult to distinguish who was supposed to be there and who was just joining in. The crowd got so involved that wrestlers from previous matches had to come on to act as security. But again this was part of the choreography of the night, an ensemble of the whole night's cast.

By the end of the fight I had lost Molly, she no doubt had some poor bastard in a headlock or had formed a gang with the kids she'd been singing with. I gathered our belongings and went to hunt her down when I bumped into Stew again.

'That was so much fun!' I said, surprised to find myself so out of breath.

'I told you wrestling was amazing,' he told me. 'Look what I got!' he said, showing me a crumpled piece of paper. 'Britani Knight's autograph!'

'Who's Britani Knight?'

'One of the fit girl wrestlers. She's over there, look.' He pointed out a girl in a white vest top, stood by herself as people filed out of the venue and back to the bar. I still had Andy's camera in my hand.

'Get a photo of us,' I said to Stew, instinctively thrusting the camera into his hands as I went to say hello to Britani. She obliged, and for the first time in my life I adopted the role of a fan, with my arm around a 'celeb' and we smiled as the camera flashed. When I was eight years old I met Princess Diana, but that was nothing compared with this. I thanked Britani for the photo and Molly joined us, similarly euphoric.

'There's Zebra!' Stew shouted, and pointed at the back of the room, where our new hero emerged from the dressing room, towel around his neck.

'We should get a photo of him too,' I said, and off the three of us went without a second thought. Moments later I had my arm around a wrestler once more. The Zebra was slightly less nubile and fragrant than Britani Knight, but it was he who had been the big attraction of the night, particularly with the children, who were up way past their bedtime, and clamouring for autographs.

'Is that blood?' a little boy asked, pointing at a scratch on the Zebra's shaved head.

'Nah, tomato ketchup,' he said, wiping it off with his fingers. By now the ring was being disassembled, time had been called at the bar and those of us who remained were asked to make our way. We said goodbye to Stew, and set off to walk back home. We were desperate for the night to continue, but it was almost midnight, Easter Sunday, and we were in Norwich, so had to resign ourselves to the fact the party was over.

At half two in the morning we were still sat at the dining table, drinking tea, eating Cadbury's Mini Eggs. We looked at the photos we'd taken on Andy's digital camera. They were incredible, snapshots of one of the strangest and most enjoyable nights I'd had for months, years even, all thanks to an advert in a newsagent's window. And not only had I been able to share it with Molly, but with Stew, the first friend I made when I moved to Norwich. It felt a long way from skulking off to Michelle's house to buy a Beaver's uniform, which still remained untouched in a plastic bag under my bed.

24

SELLING THE CAR

It was 10 a.m., the June sun shone brightly, and I'd had the most peaceful sleep since I was a baby. I opened my window fully to let fresh air in, walked through to the kitchen to pour myself a glass of orange juice then back to my room to get dressed. Suddenly a gust of wind knocked over my glass on the windowsill, juice went flying everywhere and the glass smashed into pieces on the carpet. I cut my hand picking the pieces up. In the space of five minutes I had somehow transformed from the most contented person in the world to having my bedroom carpet stained with fruit juice and blood. I stood at the sink rinsing my bleeding fingers under the cold water tap. Perhaps the day wasn't going to be as good as I'd imagined.

I had been spending a lot of time watching Pete's videos. I was almost a Pete completist, close to working my way through the entire collection, the stack of 'watched' videos in my front room was over twice as high as the 'to watch' pile. I was sat on the settee watching *Big Trouble in Little China* when I got a phone call.

'Hello?'

'Hello.' The voice was unsure, the reception shaky, the background noise almost unbearable. It sounded like the caller was standing on a runway at Heathrow or in the pit lane at Silverstone.

'Hello?' I said again, louder, but couldn't distinguish the voice at the other end. I thought about hanging up when suddenly there was clarity and a voice became audible.

'HELLO!' the voice bawled one more time, even louder, and without the background interference the words damaged my ear drums.

'I'D LIKE TO BUY YOUR CAR!'

I was so excited I paused the video.

'If it's still available?' he continued, more quietly now, having adjusted to the sound levels.

'Yes, it's still here. When are you able to come round?' I asked, attempting not to display my euphoria, trying not to reveal my desperation at getting rid of my stupid car.

'I could come now?'

Now was a problem. I was about to leave for work, I was already wearing my work clothes and was ready to get on my bike and go. But I really needed to sell the car. I wanted to be rid of the Cruel Mistress for ever. I should have had her scrapped in Bowthorpe car park when I had the opportunity. This was the last chance a member of the general public would have to own my car. If this didn't result in a sale I would have it scrapped at the weekend. Even if he offered twenty pounds I would say yes. I would accept any loose change he had in his wallet, a book of first-class stamps, his Sainsbury's Nectar card.

I was so desperate to get rid of it that if my potential buyer was in a mood to negotiate he would possibly be able to drive away with a free car and even get a bit of petrol money thrown in to help him on his way. I'd had enough.

'Now's fine,' I told him. I was happy to let him dictate. The customer is always right. Although whoever coined that particular axiom clearly never worked in the public service sector. I phoned work, told them I was unavoidably delayed and that I would get there as soon as I could. I was putting myself first, people at work could survive without me. The hotel could look after itself; I had a car to sell. I made myself a cup of tea and pressed play on the video again, watching Kurt Russell chase a few more gangs while I waited for the doorbell to ring.

Fifteen minutes later a man in a flat cap and silver beard stood on my doorstep.

'Hello, I'm Tom. We just spoke.'

'John,' I said, walking outside with him, closing the door behind me.

'Hello, John,' he said, so cheerful I thought he might give me a cuddle. He wore a cardigan and corduroy trousers and had a carrier bag with a rolled-up newspaper and vegetables inside. He had ruddy red cheeks and such a cheery disposition that he made Richard Briers look like Rose West. He followed me to where the car was parked.

'This is her,' I said, putting my hand on the bonnet of the Cruel Mistress like a dad proudly ruffling his son's hair.

'Looks in good condition,' Tom said to me. Already he was

my favourite person I'd met through newsagents' windows. 'How long have you had it?'

'Six months. She runs perfectly, I just don't need her any more.' What I lacked in technical knowledge I was compensating for with personification.

'Would it be possible to take it on a test run?' Tom asked.

'Of course.'

I wasn't sure how to do this, I didn't know who should take the role of designated driver in a test run, I've never been on one before, so I dangled the car keys for Tom to see what happened. He seemed content enough to drive, but to be fair he seemed to be having the time of his life when he was just standing on the doorstep waiting for me to open my front door. He beamed a perpetually jolly and happy smile and being in his company was as comforting as being in the womb. He took the keys from me, walked round to the driver's side, but as he climbed in I remembered an impending moment of embarrassment.

'The only problem with the car,' I said before he sat down, 'is that you can only open the passenger door from the inside.'

As Tom leant across to let me in we were both aware the asking price had just been knocked down by at least a hundred pounds. I had made the mistake Michelle had made when she pointed out that she'd biroed her son's name on the label of the Beaver's uniform.

Both of us seat-belted, Tom turned the ignition.

'Starts perfectly every time,' I said, desperately trying to recall Anthony's sales patter from six months earlier, although hopefully without slipping into his *Daily Star* patois. Tom indicated left, and we drove through the residential area and onto the main road heading out of Norwich, past the garden centre and he kept driving, onwards and onwards. I wondered whether I was going to get to work at all that afternoon.

'It's a decent car,' Tom said as we got out of the Escort outside my house half an hour later. 'I'd happily give you a hundred for it.' I wanted to bite his arm off but thought I would sit back, see whether I was able to negotiate.

'She's advertised at two hundred and eighty,' I said, but my heart wasn't really in it, I was jaded, I wanted all this to be over.

'It's not worth two eighty, son,' he said, putting me in my place. 'This will be lucky to get through its next MOT.'

'I didn't really want to go lower than two eighty.'

'I think a hundred is a much more realistic figure.'

This was not negotiation. It was two people repeating the same numbers. I reminded myself how desperate I was to get rid of the car. Tom was offering me a hundred pounds more than anyone else was likely to. He had me by the balls and unless I lowered my price he was likely to twist and squeeze. But I was reluctant to go too low, I wanted to strike a fair deal, to be able to walk away with my head held high and not just say yes to something I wanted to say no to.

'A hundred and fifty,' I suggested. Tom smiled, his rosy red cheeks made me want to make him happy.

'I could give you one twenty,' he said, and we both knew we had arrived at the magic figure. Admittedly it was much closer to his ballpark than to mine, but my concern had been to get rid of the car rather than worry about the semantics of profit and loss.

'OK, let's say one twenty,' I said.

'That's great,' Tom said, and we shook hands, smiling, as though posing for a picture for the local newspaper. As we both filled out the relevant paperwork I hoped the Cruel Mistress's new owner would have a long and happy life with the car. I think we were both pretty pleased with the deal, and I wondered whether Tom could detect my relief at the weight that had just been lifted, that I had been trapped underneath the Cruel Mistress for hours, and Tom had found us, rolled up his sleeves and lifted the car so I could crawl out. Tom took out his wallet and paid £120 from a wad of notes and I tried not to smile too broadly as they transferred from his hand to mine.

I watched him drive away and did not even feel a twinge of regret that the car was out of my life. It was pure relief. I hadn't even bothered to take the tape out of the car, I didn't want anything I associated with that part of my past. An episode of my life was over and I had learned my lesson.

I was almost two hours late for work and to my surprise found that the hotel was not on fire, it had not gone into administration. They had managed to carry on without me. For the rest of my shift that evening I was aware of the £120 in my trouser pocket and felt slightly better about life than I had done when I woke up. I looked forward to getting back home, not having to walk past my car parked outside my house, and to finishing off watching *Big Trouble in Little China*.

The next day I woke up in good spirits in the knowledge there was no longer a rusty red Escort outside with my name on its insurance. Things were looking up, and I remembered my promise that as soon as the car was sold I would stop using newsagents' windows. To celebrate I went to see Paddy at the pub he lived in. Joel answered the door.

'Paddy's been telling me about your newsagents' windows carry-on,' he said as we walked upstairs to the office. 'What other adverts have you answered?' he asked. I told him about Anthony and Chicago, and the Beaver's uniform, and that I was thinking about selling the less useful things I had acquired.

'What condition's the bike in?' he asked when I told him about John and the cat at the vet's.

'Good as new.'

'Well, I'll buy it. If you want? My last one got stolen. I'm going to buy one anyway, I may as well buy yours if you want to get rid of it.'

I wasn't sure. The bicycle was a different matter from the car; it was low maintenance and had actually been of use to me.

'Only if you don't want to keep it?' Joel reiterated. But I knew there was only one response I could give, I needed the money more than I needed the wheels and told Joel he could have it.

'It's locked up outside if you want to look,' I suggested, and hoped the Norwich bike thieves would be kind to us, not steal a bike with such heritage.

'If you say it's good I'll take your word for it. I'll give you fifty pounds for it now if you like.'

There was no way I could say no. The spirit of newsagents' windows was spreading. Joel opened up his wallet, the sound of Velcro put dollar signs in my eyes and he handed me five ten-pound notes. I liked Joel, I had known him since we were in our first year at university, and now that he was involved in what I was doing it legitimized it, somehow it started to make sense. What had been so stupid at times was now starting to benefit people. I thought about John and his cat, and wondered how both of them were since the injection at the vet's. I thought about Michelle, and her son at karate class, no doubt kicking other boys in the goolies like there was no tomorrow. I thought about Tom driving around in his red Ford Escort. I thought of Anthony preparing to set up a new life. People now had things they wanted, and it was all because of me. Well, me and newsagents' windows.

Paddy joined us.

'How's the sitcom going?' Joel asked.

'We got a rejection email this morning,' Paddy told us.

'Oh,' I said.

'Yeah.'

'Sorry guys,' Joel said.

'We never really expected anything,' I reassured him, in case he thought our worlds had just fallen apart. 'It was all about having a go, seeing whether we could do it. We'll try again another time, I'm sure. Won't we, Paddy?'

Paddy muttered something noncommittal, but the more I thought about it the more encouraged I felt. Writing the fifteen or so pages had been fun, and rejection didn't seem such a bad thing, because at least it meant we'd tried. If you don't fail from time to time it means you're not creating the chance to be lucky, for something to happen.

*

Now that the car and bike had been sold it made sense to be rid of as many items relating to newsagents' windows as possible. I had watched nearly all of the videos I had bought from Pete, so I gathered them together, put them in the cardboard banana box given to us by Mike and Donna almost a year ago, and the next day I walked to the charity shop on Unthank Road. I couldn't face the prospect of trying to sell them; I'm fairly sure nobody but me buys videos any more. Even in charity shops they seem anachronistic. I didn't want to have to write out the card or talk to a newsagent. A man came out of the charity shop and held the door open for me as I struggled with an overflowing box of VHS, all the videos apart from *An American Werewolf in London*, which I wanted to hold on to as a souvenir, my favourite film from Pete's collection.

'I'd like to donate these videos please,' I said to the woman behind the counter. The look on her face said 'I bet they need rewinding' rather than 'What a charming, generous man.'

I watched as she took them through to the back room; all of the films that I had diligently sat through, and for the most part enjoyed, and it seemed like it was the end of an era. I left the shop and looked forward to the thought of them being sold, one by one, for fifty pence each, or possibly even cheaper. What was important was that they would no longer be in my house collecting dust, reminding me of the smell of Pete's flat.

There was one more item that I still wanted to get rid of, and back at home I found an unexpected buyer.

'Can I have this?' Molly asked. She was holding the Beaver's uniform. I had taken it from under my bed that morning to try and sell. Or give away. Or burn.

'Erm, OK,' I said, slightly taken aback. Molly seemed dispro-portionately excited to have an item of such worthlessness. She gave me eight pounds, the amount I had paid Michelle.

'Souvenir,' she said, putting the jumper back in the bag, 'of the first year in our house.'

25

ANOTHER MASSAGE

When I was sorting through the videos and trying to get my house back to normal, I found the business card Massage Lucy had given me, and decided it would be a good time to get back in touch and see how the psychic massage industry was doing. It was approaching a year since I'd had the massage. Lucy had urged me to go back and make a second appointment, but I had never got round to it. It didn't seem a year since that day on Unthank Road, when I was pacing up and down trying to pluck up the courage to call her. Molly and I had been in our new house for almost a year. She still hadn't put up the purple curtains she'd bought at the garage sale – I knew she didn't like them. It isn't only me who says yes to things they want to say no to. I dialled Lucy's number and asked for an appointment.

'When would you like to come?' she asked.

'Tomorrow?' I suggested. I heard pages of her diary being turned.

'Tomorrow,' she repeated, 'I look forward to seeing you.'

Not as much as I looked forward to seeing her.

The advice Massage Lucy had given me at my previous appointment had helped to change the way I lived. She had said that I needed to release the frustration that was bubbling up inside me. And that I needed to gradually let out any anger, little by little. She had probably used the imagery of a balloon bursting. She had told me I was not decisive enough, that I needed to be more assertive, that I had no soulmate, no goals any more, and had run out of dreams.

It had all been completely true. Thanks to Massage Lucy I had been able to do something about it, correct the things in my life that weren't up to scratch, try to delay for as long as possible this inevitable breakdown she had predicted. Maybe there was a slight chance it wouldn't even happen.

I felt I had improved dramatically since I had timidly walked to her house last year. I hoped this time she would see me as a vastly improved person. I was enjoying my work at the hotel, I felt physically fitter, I didn't have any serious money problems. I thought back to that day and I knew I had been a bit of a mess. But this time Lucy was going to be opening her door to someone much less bewildered, more at ease with himself. Maybe this time I would even enjoy my massage, be able to relax and come out refreshed, re-energized.

I knocked on the door and Lucy, friendly as before, invited me in. She looked good, the colour in her cheeks and her broad smile suggested that the year had been kind to her.

'How are you?' I asked.

'Very well,' she said, and once again I was sitting on her settee. If she remembered me she did not show it.

'There are just some forms for you to fill out first,' she told me.

'Do I have to fill them out again?' I asked. 'This isn't my first time.'

'Really?'

'I've been here once before, about a year ago.' I didn't want to tell her it was precisely a year ago to the day. It may have spooked her a little.

She looked me up and down, perhaps trying to recall our paths crossing before.

'Well, it's good to have people coming back for more,' she said, and put the forms back in the folder, and instructed me to strip.

This time I had no qualms about unbuttoning my shirt, I was in better shape than I had been last year when the thought of anyone seeing my flesh made me squirm. Back then you could have pinched flab on my belly like it was the cheek of a new-born baby but those days were over, I'd been careful with what I ate, and I'd been biking to and from work ever since I met John and his cat.

I was slightly surprised that Lucy didn't remember me, but then it had only been forty-five minutes of her life, almost a year ago. She met lots of strangers in her job. And most of the time she spent with her clients they were lying on their front, and she could only see their backs. Perhaps once I took my shirt off she would remember me. But it seemed that what had been a pivotal moment for me had been a normal day at the massage table for her.

I sat on the settee as Lucy spread out her oils, applied the

Amazonian rainforest music and fetched me a glass of iced water.

'What do you do for a living?' Lucy asked as I cocked a leg over the massage table.

'I work in a hotel,' I told her.

'That sounds nice,' she said, slopping oils over my shoulders.

'It is,' I said, enjoying the sensation of her fingers on my neck, managing to locate every crick, every twinge. I had knots in my neck the shape of businessmen's suitcases.

'Is that what you want to do?' she asked.

'Not really,' I told her.

'What would you like to do?' she asked.

'I want to work abroad.' I had worked out what my dreams were.

'Ooh, me too,' Lucy said, 'I've always wanted to work abroad.'

As I closed my eyes both of us allowed our imaginations to get the better of us, and thought of drinking wine in Parisian restaurants, cycling through the Swiss countryside. I thought about Marie and Denmark, how she had taught me a different Danish word every day when I'd gone to visit her, how we'd walked along the beach, spent hours in ice-cream cafes.

My back was now covered with the slop of oils. The dribble running from the corner of my mouth, down the side of my chin and onto the pillow suggested I was relaxed. Lucy rolled me to one side to rub my waist, my hip and lower back and then laid me horizontally once more, repeating the words, 'Breathe, relax. Breathe, relax. Breathe . . .'

As I lay there I thought of all the things that had happened over the last twelve months. Lucy had told me I had no soul-mate, and that was true. Although I was now no closer to having someone I shared everything with, living with Molly and even my time with Leni had meant that I had been able to unburden myself, talk about things, have someone interested in listening to what I was saying. Lucy had said I needed to be more assertive, and I had definitely grown more so – meeting so many strangers had been good for me. I felt I was more equipped to deal with confrontation and apply my own assertiveness to situations. And although I never grabbed anyone by the throat and choked them until I got a good deal, or threatened them with the mob, I think I did pretty well. I don't know any mobs anyway.

Lucy soothed every ache in my back until they had disappeared completely and the dolphins on the stereo swam into my daydreams. The sunshine through the net curtain reminded me that summer was here and I felt relaxed and at peace with myself. I looked forward to trips to the Norfolk coast, afternoons in beer gardens. For the first time since I had moved in with Molly my bedroom was in a normal state of affairs: it had none of Pete's videos, my diary had no appointments for psychic massages or to meet a stranger in a pub to plot a sitcom. There were no more synopses for sitcoms cluttering my desk. I had no car outside my house. I had started to get a little tired of the adverts, responding to them had been fun, but I'd had enough. I was looking for friends, a soulmate, things to do in my free time. I didn't actually realize I'd had those things all along.

Soon the music had stopped and Lucy was rinsing her hands under the tap. My forty-five minutes were over, I was going to have to wake from my slumber and get back to my feet.

'How did you find that?' she asked me.

I nodded my head. 'Incredible,' I told her, with honesty. I

wanted to talk to her about the psychic massage she had given me a year ago and the impact it had had on my life.

'When I was here last time you gave me a lot of advice that I found really helpful,' I told her as I put my trousers back on. 'You told me I said yes to things I want to say no to. You said not to dwell on things that worried me.'

'Did I say those things?'

I was slightly taken aback; it seemed strange she did not remember.

'Yes, as soon as you touched my back you said you would know more about me than I knew about myself.'

'Really? That's good if it's helped you.'

I felt like I'd gone back to a different house, that I'd had a massage from the wrong person.

'Yes. You said I had unfulfilled ambitions,' I reminded her. 'You told me it's important to achieve your goals, not to let dreams go unfulfilled.'

'Well, I'm very pleased if I've been helpful,' she said. It was so frustrating, I thought seeing me again might have made her weep like an Oscar winner, but it was as though I'd never been there before, that it was the first time we had ever met.

I gave Lucy my ten pounds.

'It wouldn't hurt you to do something that scared you,' she said as I was about to close the door behind me. 'Do something that scares you,' she repeated, put the money in her purse and nodded sagely. I left Lucy's house and walked back home think-ing about all the people I had met over the last twelve months. I passed the pub where I had spent the evening with Sitcom Beth. I crossed the road and saw Sears newsagent, where I had posted and responded to so many adverts. It was the window responsible for me buying my car and Pete's videos, for going to watch the Alan Ayckbourn play. I caught sight of an image of myself in the reflection of the shop window and was happy with what I saw. I no longer had the demeanour of a broken man.

I don't know why I walked to the newsagent, whether these ubiquitous spirits had led me there or if I was guiding myself now. Surely the spirits must be getting pretty bored of me. Stood there with his hands in his pockets was an elderly man browsing the cards in the window. I walked over and stood next to him, looking to see what was being advertised. Our eyes and feet became synchronized as we shuffled along from left to right.

He walked away to a red Escort that was in even worse condition than mine had been. As he drove away I stayed where I was, on Unthank Road. A couple walked into the shop, and on their way out they stood next to me, scanning the patchwork of adverts. Neither wrote anything down or commented on anything, they just stood, reading about cars for sale and yoga lessons. It was fascinating just watching people browse; they seemed to be comforted by its presence in the same way that people like to hear the *Shipping Forecast* on Radio 4. The facts and details are irrelevant, we are just reassured that it is always there, a constant fixture in our daily lives, even though to 99 per cent of people the information is completely useless. And then I saw an advert that reminded me of the picture of domestic bliss. There was another garage sale at Mike and Donna's the next Saturday. I texted Molly and she agreed, we had to go.

I didn't know if I would place an advert again or if I would even respond to another one, but I could be certain that I would never walk past a newsagent without a smile on my face. As I walked away, I thought of all the adverts I'd seen in newsagents' windows, not just across Norwich, but the whole of Norfolk and Britain, and wondered what happened to all the lost cats.

EPILOGUE

I still had some holiday to take, so I booked two weeks off in August. As Massage Lucy had keenly noted, I still had unfulfilled ambitions, and I wanted to see what might happen. A couple of mouse clicks later and I was looking for my passport. My flight to Denmark departed in two days.

I didn't let Marie know of my plan to visit. I didn't tell anyone, I knew that if I had done they would have talked me out of it. But this was one of those situations where common sense is overrated. I just packed a bag and tiptoed to the airport. When the loudspeaker in the departure lounge announced it was time to board the flight I raised my finger to my lips and shushed. This was all a secret.

On the plane I allowed my imagination to plot a variety of outcomes. I started to imagine scenarios. Maybe I could set up my own business in Denmark teaching English. Locally I'd be known as the cool English guy with the beautiful girlfriend. We'd walk into bars and supermarkets and people would break into spontaneous applause. Maybe I would ask Marie to marry me. I would speak English to our children, Marie would speak to them in Danish, a perfectly bilingual family uniting Europe.

We'd visit family and friends in England often. Close friends would confess to me 'I'm in love with your wife' and I would nod and understand, I would not blame them. We would tell people of the day we met at a party in Vienna. We'd tell them of walking in the snow. We'd tell them how we broke up, but then I made this grand gesture and thank God I did. 'Imagine if you'd never caught that plane in secret,' Marie would say, and gasp at the prospect of spending the rest of our lives apart. I'd tell her it was all because of Massage Lucy and Leni and newsagents' windows.

It was late by the time I landed in Denmark, so I checked into a hotel a short taxi ride from the airport. The next morning I went to an Internet cafe and emailed Marie to tell her where she could find me, if she wanted to. I told her I would wait for her at the cafe by the beach, the one we'd been to every day the last time we'd seen each other.

I wasn't sure whether she would come, and wouldn't have blamed her if she had stayed away, but later that day, after almost three hours of eating vanilla and reading an airport paperback, Marie appeared. She looked at me like I was a kitten that had just avoided being squashed running across a busy road. She seemed pleased to see me, but the way she greeted me made me realize the inevitable. We went for a walk along the beach, she told me about her new job, we talked about friends we were still in touch with from Vienna. I didn't mention the marriage or our bilingual children or that we'd alternate which country we'd spend our Christmases. It wasn't long before she told me it would never work, that it wasn't meant to be. What if I moved here? I asked and she shook her head. It was the question I had wanted to ask for over a year. I had carried around this resentment; this was the frustration Lucy had tried to massage out of me. Ever since I had last been in Denmark I had been disappointed with myself for not making more of an effort, for having let Marie slip away too easily. We said goodbye and I got a taxi back to my hotel. I knew she was right, that it was just too much. And when she told me I'd meet someone new, and that there wasn't any rush, I knew she was right. On the flight back to England I didn't feel too upset. I couldn't wait to get back to Norwich. I felt upbeat, positive, because at least I'd had a go. At least I'd had a go.

ACKNOWLEDGEMENTS

I would like to express my gratitude to everyone I met through newsagents' windows, who are many more than appear in this book. Thanks also to Paul Chambers at the National Federation of Retail Newsagents for his help and insight.

For all their hard work, time and help, I would like to thank Angela Herlihy, Mike Jones, Florence Partridge, Katherine Stanton and my agent Rebecca Winfield.

For their invaluable friendship and support I would like to thank Tim Clare, Laura Dockrill, Joe Dunthorne, Chris Gomm, Chris Hicks, Patrick Lappin, Ian 'Yanny' McKenzie, Molly Naylor, Sally Roe, Joel Stickley, Ross Sutherland, Hannah Walker and Luke Wright.

Lots of love to my mum, dad and Karen.

NOTE ON THE AUTHOR

John Osborne was born in 1981 and lives in Norwich. His first book, *Radio Head*, was Book of the Week on Radio 4. He has had poetry published in the *Guardian*, the *Spectator* and the *Big Issue*, and featured on Radio 1. As a member of the poetry collective Aisle16 he has performed at festivals including Glastonbury, Latitude and the Edinburgh Fringe. He has taught in schools and universities in England, Germany and Austria. *The Newsagent's Window* is his second book.

For more information see www.aisle16.co.uk.